Seek Ye This Jesus
Seeing, Hearing, and Dwelling with God

Robert Smith

And now, I would commend you to seek this Jesus of whom the prophets and apostles have written, that the grace of God the Father, and also the Lord Jesus Christ, and the Holy Ghost, which beareth record of them, may be and abide in you forever. Amen. (Ether 12:41)

Part 1: Repent and Come to the Lord

Part 2: Walking with God

Part 1:

Repent and Come to the Lord

God is just and merciful: "Gracious is the Lord, and righteous; yea, our God is merciful." (Psalm 116:5) These two traits act together in a way that mean that while he will ensure that you will always be recompensed for the good that you do and that you become, you can also rest assured that when you make mistakes, he will forgive you the second you learn from them.

When Moses achieved this state, God showed him the nature of his character:

> 6 ...merciful and gracious, longsuffering, and abundant in goodness and truth,
> 7 Keeping mercy for thousands, forgiving iniquity and transgression and sin... (Exodus 34)

God will likewise unfold his character to you as you focus your heart and mind on him. You will have many experiences with him, each one providing you greater happiness than anything this world can offer.

You will gain great perspective and understanding regarding the unpleasant things in this world. You will experience deep meaning in life—all of life, even the day-to-day, seemingly mundane things. You will see the beauty in all of God's creations. Your compassion for others and your willingness to forgive yourself will increase. When you suffer, you will always have the Lord as an advocate—not in the sense of an imagined friend, but a tangible, real companion who will support you when no one else can. You will see miracles happen in your life on a daily basis. You will begin and end each day in overwhelming gratitude for the abundant evidences of God's love in your life.

The Lord wants you to know him. The way to do that is to accept his invitation: "Come, follow me...." (Matthew 4:19 NIV)

The Lord's way is for you to live as his servant. The Lord described his way as a yoke—a rack placed on oxen that enables them to pull a connected cart or plow. He said that his yoke is easy and his burden light.

It may seem puzzling how living his commandments—which are not always easy—and serving him always—which is sometimes quite heavy—could be described as easy or light. The secret to his pregnant statement is to consider it in the context of the world.

If it were possible to avoid the deeply painful and negative aspects of living as the world does, what would you be willing to do for that kind of relief? How much effort would you be willing to exert to gain that relief for yourself?

It turns out that what God asks of us is far easier and far lighter than the burdens of normal, worldly life. When done properly, the benefits far, far outweigh the costs, not only in terms of the sorrow that you avoid, but in terms of the positive experiences you gain.

Whether you have always believed in God, or whether you've never been given a reason to, this book will help you better understand both what God provides and why it is beneficial. It contains information you have not yet considered.

Because of the breadth of what is covered, the information is organized topically, meaning that you should not think that the contents of one chapter mean the rest of the book focuses on that subject.

Because of the complexity of the information, some ideas are mentioned only very briefly despite the fact that they are worthy of much more attention.

This book should be considered a summary. It is meant to teach you how to reach out to God and why you should. He can fill in all the gaps and take you further.

Why Now?

*For there is nothing hid, which shall not be manifested;
neither was any thing kept secret, but that it should come
abroad. (Mark 4:22)*

The purpose of this book is to help all men come to Christ through repentance and the establishment of a hearing and seeing relationship with him. This book does not contain any gimmicks or tricks. It simply contains an arrangement of the many pertinent scriptures on these topics arranged in a way to help the reader have faith to overcome whatever has kept them from the Lord to this point, whether it be sin, unbelief, false traditions, or ignorance.

This is a tall order. Christians may find themselves asking, "If the things in this book are true, why haven't I heard them before?" Non-believers may find themselves saying, "I've seen so many examples of false religion. Why should I believe this?"

The answer to these questions is simple, but perhaps dissatisfying to some. God's path is always found only by the minority of the minority. He said, "strait is the gate, and narrow is the way, which leadeth unto life, and few there be that find it." (Matthew 7:14)

The Lord delights in working mighty works through people of no apparent importance, as was evident in his own mortal ministry.

> But God hath chosen the foolish things of the world to confound the wise; and God hath chosen the weak things of the world to confound the things which are mighty; (1 Corinthians 1:27)

You may not have heard of the ideas in this book. You may find yourself wondering why you have not heard of them before. In his mortal ministry, the Savior preached markedly different ideas to Israel.

They were markedly different not because they were something new, but because the common understanding of the gospel had veered so far away from how it was originally revealed.

The truths in this book are not new. They are eternal. Throughout history, relatively few individuals have manifested the humility and diligence required to discover and apply these truths in their lives. These few have established the same kind of relationship with God that Adam and Eve enjoyed in the Garden of Eden before their fall.

These truths have always been available to all, but known to relatively few. The majority of people have been kept from them by their persistence in false tradition, a willingness to settle for less, and their love of sin.

The path to obtain these supernal truths has always included lengthy toil and great sacrifice on the part of the seeker. It may seem contrary to this pattern to neatly package a plain overview of these topics into a single book. It is important to understand why the time to publish these doctrines in plain simplicity has now come.

We live in the last days before the Second Coming of the Lord. The tribulation that precedes the Second Coming will occur during the lifetime of most of us alive today.

In the past, God could not make all truth generally accessible. To do so would lay heavy condemnation on all those who would not receive what was offered. There is a set quantity of truth and commandments appointed for all men to receive. To obtain more, men had to invest a tremendous amount of faith, obedience, and time. In days past, God would mercifully reserve the core truths of the gospel to the few who diligently searched and obeyed. After all, all those who truly seek him will find them. Giving too much to too many in too much plainness would damn them, because they would reject and be held accountable for what was revealed plainly to them. In previous times, it was better to hide more of the truth and commandments in the hope that the reprobate would, at some later phase of their lives, finally turn to God. Compared to free and open availability, the waiting period and extra effort required actually increased their chances of success.

The period in which we live is different than any period from the past. Now, in the last days, the Lord is making more and more truth and commandments plainly available. In our day, the consequences of revealing too much truth publicly are mitigated by the impending calamities that are fast approaching. Those alive today do not have long lives of peace and safety ahead of them. If they do not repent soon, they will not have the chance to repent at all. Because of his mercy, God must make more truth readily accessible because it is necessary to have to navigate the darkness that is coming.

There is a finite amount of time remaining before his return. The intervals between the increasingly destructive events God is pouring out will continue to diminish until the desolation is constant and complete. Those who do not attain a real relationship with God will not survive his return.

Christians today claim to know the God they worship. Honest Christians must admit that their experiences pale in comparison to the faithful in the scriptures. If they are honest, they must admit that there is something that has evaded them in spite of a lifetime of dedicated worship.

Non-believers, on the other hand, are awash with religious claims that fail to stand up to any serious scrutiny or close inspection. The litany of false claims and false religions makes it difficult to take seriously anyone claiming to possess the truth. As a result, God is dismissed as fake due to the many poor examples of those who claim to follow him, but fail to do the things that he did while on this earth.

In our day, believers have the opportunity to claim all the blessings recorded in the scriptures. In our day, non-believers will be given the opportunity to evaluate the gospel on its true merits. All those who love the Lord will come to know him. They will "see eye to eye, when the LORD shall bring again Zion." (Isaiah 52:8) They will either rise up to a greater relationship with God, or they will be destroyed.

The day for all mankind to rise up and know God is today. "For there is nothing hid, which shall not be manifested; neither was any thing kept secret, but that it should come abroad." (Mark 4:22) The Lord is flooding the earth with the instructions on how to achieve such a relationship. At present, this flood of truth is not generally perceived, because so few are participating in it. Rest assured that the flood of evil we see in the world today is balanced by an outpouring of light and truth from God. This book is part of that outpouring. It is not the first part, or the last part, but what it contains is critical knowledge for all who already believe in God and those who are honestly willing to consider that he might be real.

God is real, and he is knowable. If you follow the instructions he has given in scripture, you will come to know him.

An Audience with Christ

If my people, which are called by my name, shall humble themselves, and pray, and seek my face, and turn from their wicked ways; then will I hear from heaven, and will forgive their sin, and will heal their land. (2 Chronicles 7:14)

As Jesus closed out his mortal ministry, he spoke these words:

> 1 These words spake Jesus, and lifted up his eyes to heaven, and said, Father, the hour is come; glorify thy Son, that thy Son also may glorify thee:
> 2 As thou hast given him power over all flesh, that he should give eternal life to as many as thou hast given him.
> 3 And *this is life eternal, that they might know thee the only true God, and Jesus Christ, whom thou hast sent.* (John 17)

Jesus described eternal life as knowing him and the Father. Some may be tempted to interpret this scripture in a non-obvious or non-literal way. For example, some might consider that we are supposed to know God figuratively, and that we get to know him by worshipping him and studying the scriptures. Others might consider that you only know him when you die.

Reading this scripture in context of other scriptures saves us from these and other similar interpretations. John made it even clearer when he wrote: "He that hath the Son hath life; and he that hath not the Son of God hath not life." (1 John 5:12) You might be able to claim that you know someone you've never met (though that is dubious), but could you claim that you "have" someone you have never met? To have someone, they have to be with you.

The Lord Jesus *can* literally come to you. If he has not literally come to you, you do not have him. If you do not have him, you do not have eternal life.

Some believe it is not possible for God to come to you. The scriptures witness that he can, providing a litany of examples of God appearing to men. Adam saw God face to face. Enoch did as well. Jacob also saw God: "And Jacob called the name of the place Peniel: for I have seen God face to face, and my life is preserved." (Genesis 32:30) Moses and dozens of others saw God face to face.

> 9 Then went up Moses, and Aaron, Nadab, and Abihu, and seventy of the elders of Israel:
> 10 And they saw the God of Israel: and there was under his feet as it were a paved work of a sapphire stone, and as it were the body of heaven in his clearness. (Exodus 24)

The resurrected Christ appeared to hundreds of people, people who had known him well before his crucifixion.

> 1 That which was from the beginning, which we have heard, which we have seen with our eyes, which we have looked upon, and our hands have handled, of the Word of life;
> 2 (For the life was manifested, and we have seen it, and bear witness, and shew unto you that eternal life, which was with the Father, and was manifested unto us;)
> 3 That which we have seen and heard declare we unto you, that ye also may have fellowship with us: and truly our fellowship is with the Father, and with his Son Jesus Christ. (1 John 1)

Some believe that while God visited and spoke to some people in the past, it isn't something he does today. There isn't a single scripture that suggests that this is the case, and there are many that show that just the opposite is true. The Lord made this promise in the Sermon on the Mount: "Blessed are the pure in heart: for they shall see God." (Matthew 5:8) This promise and others like it did not come with an expiration date.

As wonderful as it is to see God, a visitation is only the beginning! Seeing God is still not the same as knowing God. Moses wanted all Israel to be prophets (see Numbers 11:29 and Deuteronomy 5:4). Only a few were. Prophets have not only seen and spoken with the Lord, they see him and speak with him often. Jesus said, "If a man love me, he will keep my words: and my Father will love him, and we will come unto him, and make our abode with him." (John 14:23) An abode is much more than a single visitation. If someone abides with you, you have constant access to them. To see and speak with the Lord is not meant to be a rare event. It is possible for you to hear the voice of the Lord whenever you ask him a question, to see him often, and to spend a great deal of time in his presence—all while still in this life. It is not only possible, but arriving at this point is the very purpose of your life.

God is an unchanging God. He operates today according to the same perfect attributes he has always had. He still stands at the gate to eternal life.

> O then, my beloved brethren, come unto the Lord, the Holy One. Remember that his paths are righteous. Behold, the way for man is narrow, but it lieth in a straight course before him, and the keeper of the gate is the Holy One of Israel; and he employeth no servant there; and there is none other way save it be by the gate; for he cannot be deceived, for the Lord God is his name. (2 Nephi 9:41)[1]

---

[1] I have opted to include verses from the Book of Mormon alongside verses from the Bible. The Book of Mormon is an extra-biblical book of scripture recorded between 2200 BC to 421 AD, at which time it was buried to keep it safe from dissidents seeking its destruction. In 1827, a man named Joseph Smith was led by an angel to these plates, which he translated into English by the commandment and power of God. Though many fear the Book of Mormon, an honest inspection of its contents will dispel any concern. It is a witness of Jesus Christ. It does not contradict the Bible. Believing in it does not require one to be Mormon any more than believing in the Bible requires one to be Catholic. If you are the kind of person who is not willing to consider things you have not considered before, this book is not for you—not only because you will reject the arguments made using sources you do not consider permissible, but because God is forever unknowable to

He still ministers personally to *all* who inherit salvation. Jesus is still the author and finisher of our faith (see Hebrews 12:2).

The smallness of the number of people who have obtained an audience with Christ is not due to any unwillingness on God's part, but a lack of understanding and desire on the part of his children. Hosea described the two reasons that believers have not yet seen the face of the Lord:

> 6 They shall go with their flocks and with their herds to seek the Lord; but they shall not find him; he hath withdrawn himself from them.
> 9 Ephraim shall be desolate in the day of rebuke: among the tribes of Israel have I made known that which shall surely be...
> 15 I will go and return to my place, till they acknowledge their offence, and seek my face: in their affliction they will seek me early. (Hosea 5)

Believers who have not seen the Lord are practicing one or both of Hosea's conditions. Either they are sinning, they are not seeking God, or both.

No amount of self-applied labels, scriptural wresting, or pastoral assurance can make up for the plainness of this argument: if you have not yet had an audience with Christ, you have not yet qualified for eternal life. Even seeing God is just the start of the relationship required to get to know God. While sobering, this conclusion need not be depressing. You cannot improve upon a situation until you first realize it stands in need of improvement.

If you do not find yourself in possession of eternal life in the presence of God, you must conclude that you are either unaware of the instructions in the scriptures on these topics, you have not applied them, or you are mistaken in your understanding of what they are or what it means to live them.

The rest of the chapters in this book describe the process of obtaining not only an audience with Christ, but a habitation with him.

---

those who think they already know it all. If you truly know it all, you have no need for this book's purpose, because you already know God. If you haven't yet met him, perhaps you should reconsider your position.

That process begins with an understanding of repentance grounded in the particulars of the fall of Adam and Eve.

After repentance, you are ready to learn how to interact with God in ways that you have only read about. You will come to understand how it is possible to come to know God while still in this life. You will comprehend what great things God has designed in this life for those who love him.

If you follow the instructions given in the scriptures on these topics, you will find yourself in possession of eternal life in the presence of God.

Terrible or Glorious?

Christians believe they will go to heaven to live with God. It seems a foregone conclusion that their faith has prepared them to meet him. But how do they know? Do the scriptures give them a reason for this expectation? How do they describe this meeting?

We know that all mankind will inescapably come face to face with God. "For it is written, As I live, saith the Lord, every knee shall bow to me, and every tongue shall confess to God. So then every one of us shall give account of himself to God." (Romans 14:11-12)

We would like to think that this experience will be one of inexpressible joy. Some scriptures describe this sort of encounter. The Psalmist wrote, "Thou wilt shew me the path of life: in thy presence is fulness of joy; *at thy right hand there are pleasures for evermore*." (Psalm 16:11)

We read that the presence of the Lord is a place of compassion so lovely that it makes up for even the worst hardships endured in life. Heaven is a place where God wipes away the tears of his children: "For the Lamb which is in the midst of the throne shall feed them, and shall lead them unto living fountains of waters: and *God shall wipe away all tears from their eyes*." (Revelation 7:17)

There will be no more pain there:

> And God shall wipe away all tears from their eyes; and *there shall be no more death, neither sorrow, nor crying, neither shall there be any more pain:* for the former things are passed away." (Revelation 21:4)

Will all mankind experience joy in God's presence? It turns out that, on the whole, only a few descriptions of this encounter are positive. We are told that there will be two types of experiences in that day: one positive, and one negative. The negative experience is just as intense as the positive:

> 10 The same shall drink of the wine of the wrath of God, which is poured out without mixture into the cup of his indignation; and he shall be tormented with fire and brimstone in the presence of the holy angels, and in the presence of the Lamb:
> 11 And the smoke of their torment ascendeth up for ever and ever: and they have no rest day nor night... (Revelation 14)

For some, being in the presence of the holy angels and the Lord will cause torment so great that it is akin to being burned alive. This description might seem overly harsh to those who have only been exposed to the popular (yet incorrect) description of a heavenly encounter.

The key to understanding both the gravity of the negative experience and the reason for it is to understand that man's default position with God is one of separation due to sin: "For all have sinned, and come short of the glory of God;" (Romans 3:23) Some rightly understand that man was cast out of God's presence because of the fall of Adam. However, the sacrifice of Jesus Christ absolves all men of the fall of Adam:

> 14 And thus we see that all mankind were fallen, and they were in the grasp of justice; yea, the justice of God, which consigned them forever to be cut off from his presence.
> 15 And now, the plan of mercy could not be brought about except an atonement should be made; therefore God himself atoneth for the sins of the world, to bring about the plan of mercy, to appease the demands of justice, that God might be a perfect, just God, and a merciful God also. (Alma 42)

Although all mankind is redeemed from Adam's fall through the sacrifice of Jesus Christ, the fall created an environment where each individual is capable of sin: "…because of the fall our natures have become evil continually;" (Ether 3:2) Each individual has sinned, and therefore each individual is separated from God.

Our separation from God, then, is not arbitrary. It comes as a direct consequence of an individual's sin. Preparing for a reunion with God requires removing the cause of the separation. This life is given as a time to prepare to meet God, yet few understand how to prepare, and even fewer are actually preparing.

> 45 O, my beloved brethren, turn away from your sins; shake off the chains of him that would bind you fast; come unto that God who is the rock of your salvation.
> 46 Prepare your souls for that glorious day when justice shall be administered unto the righteous, even the day of judgment, that ye may not shrink with awful fear; that ye may not remember your awful guilt in perfectness, and be constrained to exclaim: Holy, holy are thy judgments, O Lord God Almighty—but I know my guilt; I transgressed thy law, and my transgressions are mine; and the devil hath obtained me, that I am a prey to his awful misery. (2 Nephi 9)

What happens to those who are not prepared? To be brought into God's presence before preparing oneself for the experience would be catastrophic. A fallen individual would not experience joy if brought into God's presence. They would instead feel indescribable pain.

> Yea, every knee shall bow, and every tongue confess before him. Yea, even at the last day, when all men shall stand to be judged of him, then shall they confess that he is God; then shall they confess, who live without God in the world, that the judgment of an everlasting punishment is just upon them; and they shall quake, and tremble, and shrink beneath the glance of his all-searching eye. (Mosiah 27:31. See also Romans 14:11 and Isaiah 45:23)

How great is the discomfort of those unprepared to see God? John describes how men will pray for rocks to fall upon them to hide themselves from God's face (see Revelation 6:16). Isaiah says men will flee into caves to avoid his presence (see Isaiah 2:19).

In life, we escape from a true understanding of our uncleanness and our nakedness by ignoring it. We fool ourselves. We pay less attention to the bad in us than we do the good. We pretend that our motives are better than they are. We claim that we aren't to blame for our faults. At that day, there will be no deception and no excuses. All men will receive a perfect knowledge at that day, a complete and correct understanding of their own works. The scriptures refer to this clarity in conjunction with God's ability to see us as we really are.

> 4 The LORD is in his holy temple, the LORD'S throne is in heaven: his eyes behold, his eyelids try, the children of men.
> 5 The LORD trieth the righteous: but the wicked and him that loveth violence his soul hateth. (Psalm 11)

You and I will stand before God, and we will see as we are seen—we will have a perfectly clear understanding of our character: our thoughts, our words, our deeds, and our desires. Standing boldly in contrast to our gross imperfection will be God, in equally clear, undeniable perfection.

We will be overwhelmed by a perfect knowledge of our own impurity in contrast to God's perfection.

> 3 Then will ye longer deny the Christ, or can ye behold the Lamb of God? Do ye suppose that ye shall dwell with him under a consciousness of your guilt? Do ye suppose that ye could be happy to dwell with that holy Being, when your souls are racked with a consciousness of guilt that ye have ever abused his laws?
> 4 Behold, I say unto you that ye would be more miserable to dwell with a holy and just God, under a consciousness of your filthiness before him, than ye would to dwell with the damned souls in hell.
> 5 For behold, when ye shall be brought to see your nakedness before God, and also the glory of God, and the holiness of Jesus Christ, it will kindle a flame of unquenchable fire upon you. (Mormon 9)

That contrast is what fills us with burning torment. The wicked will feel indescribable anguish under the full weight of their guilt, uncleanness, and nakedness. The wicked will be in agony in the presence of God because of the

> …awful view of their own guilt and abominations, which doth cause them to shrink from the presence of the Lord into a state of misery and endless torment, from whence they can no more return; therefore they have drunk damnation to their own souls. (Mosiah 3:25)

The knowledge we will receive in the presence of God will cause pain to the degree that we are not reconciled to God. Though we will comprehend his perfect love for us and his perfect righteousness, we will also "…have a perfect knowledge of all our guilt, and our uncleanness, and our nakedness…" (2 Nephi 9:14) Though Christ stands as our judge, man is his own tormentor.

After death, the wicked are "consigned to partake of the fruits of their labors or their works, which have been evil; and they drink the dregs of a bitter cup." (Alma 40:26)

> 7 For behold, after ye have been nourished by the good word of God all the day long, will ye bring forth evil fruit, that ye must be hewn down and cast into the fire?
> 8 Behold, will ye reject these words? Will ye reject the words of the prophets; and will ye reject all the words which have been spoken concerning Christ, after so many have spoken concerning him; and deny the good word of Christ, and the power of God, and the gift of the Holy Ghost, and quench the Holy Spirit, and make a mock of the great plan of redemption, which hath been laid for you?
> 9 Know ye not that if ye will do these things, that the power of the redemption and the resurrection, which is in Christ, will bring you to stand with shame and awful guilt before the bar of God?
> 10 And according to the power of justice, for justice cannot be denied, ye must go away into that lake of fire and brimstone, whose flames are unquenchable, and

whose smoke ascendeth up forever and ever, which lake of fire and brimstone is endless torment.

11 O then, my beloved brethren, repent ye, and enter in at the strait gate, and continue in the way which is narrow, until ye shall obtain eternal life. (Jacob 6)

Most Christians, believing they are not wicked, expect a different experience than this. They believe that they are righteous, and will therefore have a glorious experience when they meet God.

Remember that "wicked" doesn't always mean evil. It means those who deviate from God's law. Some deviate from God's law knowing full well what they are up to, convincing themselves that God will wink at their sin. Others deviate from God's law unknowingly, having been persuaded by their religious teachers to follow erroneous doctrine. The scriptures indicate that there will be many believers in that day who will be surprised at their experience in the presence of the Lord:

> *Not every one that saith unto me, Lord, Lord, shall enter into the kingdom of heaven;* but he that doeth the will of my Father which is in heaven. Many will say to me in that day, Lord, Lord, have we not prophesied in thy name? and in thy name have cast out devils? and in thy name done many wonderful works? And then will I profess unto them, *I never knew you:* depart from me, ye that work iniquity. (Matthew 7:21-23)

> Then said one unto him, Lord, are there few that be saved? And he said unto them, strive to enter in at the strait gate: for *many, I say unto you, will seek to enter in, and shall not be able.* When once the master of the house is risen up, and hath shut to the door, and ye begin to stand without, and to knock at the door, saying, Lord, Lord, open unto us; and he shall answer and say unto you, I know you not whence ye are: Then shall ye begin to say, We have eaten and drunk in thy presence, and thou hast taught in our streets. But he shall say, I tell you, I know you not whence ye are; depart from me, all ye workers of iniquity. There shall be weeping and gnashing of teeth, when ye shall see Abraham, and Isaac, and Jacob, and all

the prophets, in the kingdom of God, *and you yourselves thrust out.* (Luke 13:23-28)

How can you know which experience will be yours? The forgoing scriptures give the key: "he that doeth the will of my Father which is in heaven" will have a positive experience, and "workers of iniquity" will not. It would be nice to think that if you are engaged in religious practices, and if you can trace your practices to scripture, you are safe. Yet, those who rejected the Lord in his mortal ministry were also very religious, and prided themselves in their understanding of the scriptures.

Luckily, the Lord has given us certifiable proof as to whether we are doing the will of God or not:

> He that hath my commandments, and keepeth them, he it is that loveth me; and he that loveth me shall be loved of my Father, and I will love him, and will manifest myself to him. (John 14:21)

How can you know which experience will be yours? There is no need to wonder. If you are keeping God's commandments, you are prepared to meet him. If you are keeping God's commandments, God will manifest himself to you. If you have not yet met him, you are not keeping his commandments, and you are not prepared to meet him. If you are not capable of meeting him in this life, it is because you cannot stand in his presence without being consumed by pain unto death. If you cannot stand in his presence without being consumed by pain here, what awaits you when you unavoidably stand in his presence to be judged when you die, possessing a resurrected body that cannot die?

The point of religion is to bring you back into God's presence. If that has not happened despite your dutiful fulfillment of your religion, your religion is inadequate. It would be extremely foolish to assume—without any scripture indicating so—that death will magically remove the consequence of sin in your life.

> Ye cannot say, when ye are brought to that awful crisis, that I will repent, that I will return to my God. Nay, ye cannot say this; for that same spirit which doth possess your bodies at the time that ye go out of this life, that

same spirit will have power to possess your body in that eternal world. (Alma 34:34)

Instead, you ought to assume that there are key doctrines missing from your religious practice. You ought to assume you are off track in your understanding or application of Christianity.

All men, no matter their degree of righteousness, will one day see Jesus Christ with a perfect understanding of his perfection and their lack thereof. Let us prepare to abide the day so that the reunion might be one of joy and glory rather than agony and terror.

Saved From What?

And thus cometh about the salvation and the redemption of men, and also their destruction and misery. (Alma 42:26)

From what are we saved? This is the key question to ask if one is to understand the gospel of Jesus Christ, what he lived and died for, and how we are to live.

We are saved from the consequences of the fall, meaning the fall of Adam and Eve. In the beginning, this earth was free from sin. Everything created by God obeyed God's law. That all changed when Adam and Eve transgressed in Eden.

As a result of eating the fruit of knowledge of good and evil, Adam and Eve were cast out of the garden. Adam was cursed to farm against the thorns and weeds of the earth, and Eve was cursed to suffer in pregnancy and childbirth. Yet, these were only the temporal consequences of the fall. The spiritual effects of the fall were that Adam and Eve were cast out of God's presence for their sin, and knowing good from evil, were capable of more sin. The spiritual effects, like the temporal ones, were passed down to their posterity.

Being saved is broadly defined as reversing the two consequences of the fall, death and sin:

> 6 But behold, it was appointed unto man to die…and man became lost forever, yea, they became fallen man.
> 7 And now, ye see by this that our first parents were cut off both temporally and spiritually from the presence of the Lord; and thus we see they became subjects to follow after their own will. (Alma 42)

22

Both of these consequences of the fall keep men out of the presence of God: "...the fall...brought upon all mankind a spiritual death as well as a temporal, that is, they were cut off from the presence of the Lord..." (Alma 42:9)

The Lord told Adam that if he ate the fruit of the tree of knowledge, he would die (see Genesis 3:3). He ate, and in doing so, brought sin and death into the world.

Death, a consequence of the fall, is more of a blessing than a curse in the context of sin, the other consequence of the fall. Death allows a parting with our old bodies, which are tainted with sin, to take up new bodies that are not corrupted by this earth.

> 42 So also is the resurrection of the dead. It is sown in corruption; it is raised in incorruption:
> 43 It is sown in dishonour; it is raised in glory: it is sown in weakness; it is raised in power:
> 44 It is sown a natural body; it is raised a spiritual body. There is a natural body, and there is a spiritual body.
> 45 And so it is written, The first man Adam was made a living soul; the last Adam was made a quickening spirit.
> 50 Now this I say, brethren, that flesh and blood cannot inherit the kingdom of God; neither doth corruption inherit incorruption. (1 Corinthians 15)

> Even this mortal shall put on immortality, and this corruption shall put on incorruption, and shall be brought to stand before the bar of God, to be judged of him according to their works whether they be good or whether they be evil—(Mosiah 16:10)

Jesus Christ overcame physical death. He came to take away the consequence of physical death levied against Adam and Eve in the garden of Eden. The sacrifice of Jesus unconditionally takes away the penalty of death from all men through the universal resurrection.

> And if Christ had not risen from the dead, or have broken the bands of death that the grave should have no victory, and that death should have no sting, there could have been no resurrection. (Mosiah 16:7)

Now, there is a death which is called a temporal death; and the death of Christ shall loose the bands of this temporal death, that all shall be raised from this temporal death. (Alma 11:42)

Though men still die, they will be resurrected. The resurrection could not occur without Jesus having come to earth to live a perfect mortal life, thereby gaining the right to absolve humanity of physical death without violating God's perfect justice.

The second death is the term used to refer to the consequences of individual sin. In the initial state of the garden of Eden, there was no knowledge of good and evil. The fall created an environment where men tended toward sin:

Therefore, as they had become carnal, sensual, and devilish, by nature, this probationary state became a state for them to prepare; it became a preparatory state. (Alma 12:10)

Without Jesus, there would be no way to recover from the sins committed in this life:

11 And now remember, my son, if it were not for the plan of redemption, (laying it aside) as soon as they were dead their souls were miserable, being cut off from the presence of the Lord.
12 And now, there was no means to reclaim men from this fallen state, which man had brought upon himself because of his own disobedience;
15 And now, the plan of mercy could not be brought about except an atonement should be made; therefore God himself atoneth for the sins of the world, to bring about the plan of mercy, to appease the demands of justice, that God might be a perfect, just God, and a merciful God also. (Alma 42)

Without redemption through Jesus Christ, men would be forever exiled from God's presence due to their own sins: "And thus we see that all mankind were fallen, and they were in the grasp of justice; yea, the justice of God, which consigned them forever to be cut off from his presence." (Alma 42:14) As Paul explained it, "by one man sin entered into the world, and death by sin; and so death passed upon all men, for that all have sinned:" (Romans 5:12)

To experience more joy, it is necessary to acquire greater knowledge. The purpose of the gospel is to impart knowledge to men. We acquire greater knowledge as we learn to choose good over evil in increasingly difficult situations. Opposition is required to create difficult situations. Without this opposition, it becomes easy to choose good over evil, but the choice is vacuous and not beneficial.

> For it must needs be, that there is an opposition in all things. If not so, my firstborn in the wilderness, righteousness could not be brought to pass, neither wickedness, neither holiness nor misery, neither good nor bad. Wherefore, all things must needs be a compound in one; wherefore, if it should be one body it must needs remain as dead, having no life neither death, nor corruption nor incorruption, happiness nor misery, neither sense nor insensibility. (2 Nephi 2:11)

In Eden, without that opposition, mankind's ability to commit sin was incomparably attenuated compared to the environment in which we live, but so was their ability to acquire knowledge.

> 23 ...they would have remained in a state of innocence, having no joy, for they knew no misery; doing no good, for they knew no sin.
> 24 But behold, all things have been done in the wisdom of him who knoweth all things.
> 25 Adam fell that men might be; and men are, that they might have joy. (2 Nephi 2)

In the post-fall world, we have abundant opportunities to choose carnality or spirituality, sin or obedience, Satan or God, and death or life.

This environment is precisely what is needed for men to become more capable of living in God's presence. Living in God's presence requires the acquisition of more knowledge than you currently possess. Since God reveals to us as much as we are able to bear, what you do not already know is necessarily beyond your capacity to obey. Therefore, until your faith in God becomes unshakeable, acquisition of further light and truth will involve transgression. Our environment here provides the opportunity to recover from these sins in a way that does not affect our eternal state.

We all sin and experience the natural consequence of sin, "remorse of conscience unto man." (Alma 42:18) Knowledge of transgression of God's law causes men to feel gross discomfort in the presence of God.

Jesus Christ provides the missing ingredient: a way to both learn greater knowledge *and* recover from failures in the attempt:

> 22 But there is a law given, and a punishment affixed, and a repentance granted; which repentance, mercy claimeth; otherwise, justice claimeth the creature and executeth the law, and the law inflicteth the punishment...
> 23 ...mercy claimeth the penitent, and mercy cometh because of the atonement; and the atonement bringeth to pass the resurrection of the dead; and the resurrection of the dead bringeth back men into the presence of God; and thus they are restored into his presence, to be judged according to their works, according to the law and justice. (Alma 42)

Overcoming the second death is how we come back into the presence of Jesus, and how we are saved.

> 32 Therefore God gave unto them commandments, after having made known unto them the plan of redemption, that they should not do evil, the penalty thereof being a second death, which was an everlasting death as to things pertaining unto righteousness; for on such the plan of redemption could have no power, for the works of justice could not be destroyed, according to the supreme goodness of God.
> 33 But God did call on men, in the name of his Son, (this being the plan of redemption which was laid) saying: If ye will repent, and harden not your hearts, then will I have mercy upon you, through mine Only Begotten Son;
> 34 Therefore, whosoever repenteth, and hardeneth not his heart, he shall have claim on mercy through mine

Only Begotten Son, unto a remission of his sins; and these shall enter into my rest.

35 And whosoever will harden his heart and will do iniquity, behold, I swear in my wrath that he shall not enter into my rest. (Alma 12)

The plan of redemption is the focus of Part 1, and will be explained via subtopics in the remaining chapters.

The fall of Adam created the environment necessary for men to obtain greater joy and dwell in God's presence. Jesus Christ redeems men from the first death through the universal resurrection and provides a way for them to be saved from the second death.

26 And the Messiah cometh in the fulness of time, that he may redeem the children of men from the fall. And because that they are redeemed from the fall they have become free forever, knowing good from evil; to act for themselves and not to be acted upon, save it be by the punishment of the law at the great and last day, according to the commandments which God hath given. 27 Wherefore, men are free according to the flesh; and all things are given them which are expedient unto man. And they are free to choose liberty and eternal life, through the great Mediator of all men, or to choose captivity and death, according to the captivity and power of the devil; for he seeketh that all men might be miserable like unto himself.

28 And now, my sons, I would that ye should look to the great Mediator, and hearken unto his great commandments; and be faithful unto his words, and choose eternal life, according to the will of his Holy Spirit;

29 And not choose eternal death, according to the will of the flesh and the evil which is therein, which giveth the spirit of the devil power to captivate, to bring you down to hell, that he may reign over you in his own kingdom. (2 Nephi 2)

Because men are redeemed from the first death, they are provided an opportunity to choose eternal life by keeping his commandments, or to choose eternal death, which consists of remaining outside of his presence.

Is Belief Enough?

---

*...believe that ye must repent of your sins and forsake
them, and humble yourselves before God; and ask in
sincerity of heart that he would forgive you; and now, if
you believe all these things see that ye do them. (Mosiah
4:10)*

Salvation is not possible without God freely giving us what we
do not deserve. This concept is called *grace*. "For by grace are ye saved
through faith; and that not of yourselves: it is the gift of God:"
(Ephesians 2:8) It is indisputable that God freely gave the sacrifice of
Jesus Christ. Does this mean that everyone is automatically saved, or
that salvation is easy?

Myth 1: Salvation is automatic.

Some claim that all men are saved. This argument hinges on
words and phrases like "saved by grace" and "salvation is free." While
these words and phrases are found in the scriptures, when placed in
context of the body of scripture, there is no argument for automatic
salvation.

Grace requires faith, and cannot therefore be automatic. If
salvation did not require any action from us, then everyone would be
saved, and no one would be separated from God. Yet very few people
in this world *are* saved, as evidenced by several observations. First, very
few people have had an audience with God. Second, Jesus himself
indicated that few will be saved: "Because strait is the gate, and narrow
is the way, which leadeth unto life, and few there be that find it."
(Matthew 7:14)

The biggest problem with the doctrine of "free salvation" is that
its believers have absolutely no reason to change. They can continue to

disobey God with blatant disregard. In doing so, they are perpetuating their alienation from God and voiding the purpose of this life—to prepare to meet God by correcting the conditions that caused individual separation from him.

In order to reconcile the obvious contradictions between "free salvation" and God's word, proponents seem to have contrived an arbitrary God who saves some few for no particular reason, and damns all others.

If we will be so foolish as to impose a doctrine upon God, we ought to at least ensure that whatever we concoct is consistent with God's rarely disputed attributes: He is all-knowing, perfectly just, and perfectly merciful. The doctrine of automatic salvation for the arbitrary few is not just by any shade. Since God is just, automatic salvation cannot be true.

While salvation from death is free, salvation from individual sin is not.

> 8 For by grace are ye saved through faith; and that not of yourselves: it is the gift of God:
> 9 Not of works, lest any man should boast.
> 10 For we are his workmanship, created in Christ Jesus *unto good works, which God hath before ordained that we should walk in them.* (Ephesians 2:8-10)

The scriptures teach that we are saved by grace only after all we can do:

> For we labor diligently to write, to persuade our children, and also our brethren, to believe in Christ, and to be reconciled to God; for we know that it is by grace that we are saved, after all we can do. (2 Nephi 25:23)

In other words, grace is *free*, and grace is *necessary*, but grace is not *sufficient* when we deviate from its scriptural meaning and instead use it to refer to something independent of our own faith and works. Real grace—scriptural grace—is conditional. It comes from God and is a result of his goodness and glory, but always includes the heart, mind, and might of the individual. Without grace, man could not be saved from his sins, because without Jesus there would be no way of obtaining forgiveness from those sins. Yet, even with grace, man cannot be saved without actually doing what God says.

> 3 And hereby we do know that we know him, if we keep his commandments.
> 4 He that saith, I know him, and keepeth not his commandments, is a liar, and the truth is not in him.
> 5 But whoso keepeth his word, in him verily is the love of God perfected: hereby know we that we are in him.
> 6 He that saith he abideth in him ought himself also so to walk, even as he walked. (1 John 2)

Although professed believers are probably truthfully expressing that they believe in *something*, they cannot actually believe in *God* without doing his works. If you believe in God, you will accept God's grace and perform good works.

When most professed believers say *belief*, what they actually mean is *wishing*. They look at God as a genie who will do what they say, rather than a deity to whom they must submit. They *wish* that God would save them without them having to believe him by doing what he says. If what they actually meant was belief as defined by the scriptures, belief in Christ would indeed be sufficient to save.

Professed believers in God who don't actually obey God are not new. Paul wrote of them in his day: "They profess that they know God; but in works they deny him, being abominable, and disobedient, and unto every good work reprobate." (Titus 1:16)

If you believe in God, you will actually keep his commandments.

Myth 2: Salvation is easy.

If salvation isn't automatic, is it easy? Is real faith or real belief easy? Recall the man who brought his sick child to Jesus,

> 23 Jesus said unto him, If thou canst believe, all things are possible to him that believeth.
> 24 And straightway the father of the child cried out, and said with tears, Lord, I believe; help thou mine unbelief.
> 27 But Jesus took him by the hand, and lifted him up; and he arose. (Mark 9)

This man's child was in grave danger, and he had witnessed Jesus perform countless miracles. Still, he had to plead with Jesus to help him obtain sufficient faith for his child to be healed. The man required faith, and it was not easy to obtain.

We tend to overlay our current understanding and behavior onto gospel topics like grace, faith, and belief. "Faith" means much more than our common understanding, "grace" is not as easily obtained as we might like to think, and "belief" is a much deeper and difficult-to-exercise concept than we assume.

Consider the belief of Simon the sorcerer:

> 18 And when Simon saw that through laying on of the apostles' hands the Holy Ghost was given, he offered them money,
> 19 Saying, Give me also this power, that on whomsoever I lay hands, he may receive the Holy Ghost.
> 20 But Peter said unto him, Thy money perish with thee, because thou hast thought that the gift of God may be purchased with money.
> 21 Thou hast neither part nor lot in this matter: for thy heart is not right in the sight of God.
> 22 Repent therefore of this thy wickedness, and pray God, if perhaps the thought of thine heart may be forgiven thee.
> 23 For I perceive that thou art in the gall of bitterness, and in the bond of iniquity. (Acts 8)

As we see, Simon recognized God's power in Peter, and he was willing to pay good money for it. But believing in God's power is not enough.

Belief in God is an all-or-nothing proposition. Any part of him that we reject will cut us off from salvation. Simon was willing to believe in God's power, but not in his character. God's power does not exist independent of the kind of being he is—the laws he chooses to live. Without becoming like God in character, one cannot become like God in power.

Because Simon's heart was not right, he was not able to acquire the power of God. It is possible, then, to both believe in God's power and still be cut off by your wickedness, leaving you "in the gall of bitterness, and in the bond of iniquity."

Proponents of "saved by belief" proclaim that you can believe in God's power to save while disbelieving everything else about him. They posit that God can arbitrarily change a sinner to a saint, and will do so for anyone who simply confesses him. Some believe in a slightly modified version of the belief-only doctrine, which is the ordinance-only or sacrament-only doctrine. Under this mantra, God will save those who participate in a list of ordinances (sacraments).

"Saved by belief" and its variants do not require a fallen man to change. Instead, they suppose that either a man can live with God as he is, or that God will magically and forcefully change sinners into saints if they fulfill some minimal criteria.

The idea that you can somehow believe in God's power to save while disbelieving his words is ludicrous. Holistic belief in God will definitely save you, but salvation-by-belief is not believing in God. Rather, it's an attempt to believe *in* God without *believing* God. This is not *belief* as defined in the scriptures. Instead, it is an attempt to claim the blessings promised without obeying the instructions they are predicated upon. If we are saved by this kind of belief, then we are saved independent of whether or not we sin. This kind of belief in God is man-made.

Salvation-by-belief is believing in the *idea* of God without believing in the *effect* of God. We must believe in both. God saves us not through arbitrary favor, but through making us holy—and not against our will. When we become holy through obeying him, we become able to abide in his holy presence.

With so many differing beliefs out there, and God's indication that many who believe in him are not actually saved, we ought to exercise great caution in our belief systems. We ought to seek to believe God. Believing God means that we seek out and reconcile ourselves to what he has actually said, not to what we would like to think he has said. It means that we trust him enough to do what he says. It means that we interpret any lack of promised blessings as a signal that our faith is off course.

Jesus will not save anyone who does not obey him. "And he cometh into the world that he may save all men if they will hearken unto his voice;" (2 Nephi 9:21) God can save us *from* our sins, but he cannot save us *in* our sins.

> And I say unto you again that [God] cannot save them in their sins; for I cannot deny his word, and he hath said that no unclean thing can inherit the kingdom of heaven; therefore, how can ye be saved, except ye inherit the

kingdom of heaven? Therefore, ye cannot be saved in your sins. (Alma 11:37)

You can claim to believe in Jesus, but until you actually do what he says, your claim is hollow.

> And why call ye me, Lord, Lord, and do not the things which I say? (Luke 6:46)

> For he hath answered the ends of the law, and *he claimeth all those who have faith in him; and they who have faith in him will cleave unto every good thing;* wherefore he advocateth the cause of the children of men; and he dwelleth eternally in the heavens. (Moroni 7:28)

Those who truly believe God will keep his commandments.

> 3 For *this is the love of God,* that *we keep his commandments:* and his commandments are not grievous.
> 4 For whatsoever is born of God overcometh the world: and this is the victory that overcometh the world, even our faith.
> 5 *Who is he that overcometh the world, but he that believeth that Jesus is the Son of God?* (1 John 5)

Much of the confusion comes from a conflation of forgiveness and salvation. Forgiveness of sin is free for all who sincerely ask:

> Let the wicked forsake his way, and the unrighteous man his thoughts: and let him return unto the Lord, and he will have mercy upon him; and to our God, for he will abundantly pardon. (Isaiah 55:7)

However, obtaining forgiveness is not the same as being saved. To be saved from the effects of the fall, you must change your character, habits, and desires. Forgiveness of sins absolves you from penalty of past sins, but it does not make you any less capable of committing future sin. It makes you clean, but not holy.

Those who do not forsake their sins gain nothing from asking forgiveness: "He that covereth his sins shall not prosper: but whoso confesseth *and forsaketh* them shall have mercy." (Proverbs 28:13) Those who continue in sin despite being taught God's commandments do not believe God, but are in open rebellion against God, and are not saved.

> 37 I say unto you, that the man that [sins], the same cometh out in open rebellion against God; therefore he listeth to obey the evil spirit, and becometh an enemy to all righteousness; therefore, the Lord has no place in him, for he dwelleth not in unholy temples.
> 38 Therefore if that man repenteth not, and remaineth and dieth an enemy to God, the demands of divine justice do awaken his immortal soul to a lively sense of his own guilt, which doth cause him to shrink from the presence of the Lord, and doth fill his breast with guilt, and pain, and anguish, which is like an unquenchable fire, whose flame ascendeth up forever and ever.
> 39 And now I say unto you, that mercy hath no claim on that man; therefore his final doom is to endure a never-ending torment. (Mosiah 2)

Belief in God of itself doesn't remove an individual's tendency to sin. The devils believe in God, but that hasn't saved them: "Thou believest that there is one God; thou doest well: the devils also believe, and tremble." (James 2:19). This is further proven by the abundant examples of self-professed Christians who live ungodly lives. God's purpose is not to incite shallow claims of belief from his children. Instead, his purpose is to give us the opportunity to become more like he is so that we can enjoy more of the blessings he has. Good works don't spontaneously appear through divine intervention in the lives of believers.

Without changing your desires, you will continue to commit the same sins for which you have asked forgiveness. In the presence of God, there is no difference between one who *has* committed sin and one who *can* commit sin. The Lord said that those who desire to commit sin are guilty of sin: "But I say unto you, That whosoever looketh on a woman to lust after her hath committed adultery with her already in his heart." (Matthew 5:28)

Recognizing that confession of Christ has not changed their behavior, some believe that while their belief may not change them presently, it does qualify them to dwell with God hereafter. Does death change your capacity for sin? Did birth separate you from God, or did sin? If sin separates you from God, why would death reunite you with him?

Death does not change your relationship with God. The scriptures clearly teach that death does not change your character. As a godly man once taught his son:

> 2 I say unto thee, my son, that the plan of restoration is requisite with the justice of God; for it is requisite that all things should be restored to their proper order. Behold, it is requisite and just, according to the power and resurrection of Christ, that the soul of man should be restored to its body, and that every part of the body should be restored to itself.
>
> 3 And it is requisite with the justice of God that men should be judged according to their works; and if their works were good in this life, and the desires of their hearts were good, that they should also, at the last day, be restored unto that which is good.
>
> 4 And if their works are evil they shall be restored unto them for evil. Therefore, all things shall be restored to their proper order, every thing to its natural frame—mortality raised to immortality, corruption to incorruption—raised to endless happiness to inherit the kingdom of God, or to endless misery to inherit the kingdom of the devil, the one on one hand, the other on the other—
>
> 5 The one raised to happiness according to his desires of happiness, or good according to his desires of good; and the other to evil according to his desires of evil; for as he has desired to do evil all the day long even so shall he have his reward of evil when the night cometh.
>
> 6 And so it is on the other hand. If he hath repented of his sins, and desired righteousness until the end of his days, even so he shall be rewarded unto righteousness.
>
> 7 These are they that are redeemed of the Lord; yea, these are they that are taken out, that are delivered from that endless night of darkness; and thus they stand or fall; for behold, they are their own judges, whether to do good or do evil.

8 Now, the decrees of God are unalterable; therefore, the way is prepared that whosoever will may walk therein and be saved.

9 And now behold, my son, do not risk one more offense against your God upon those points of doctrine, which ye have hitherto risked to commit sin.

10 Do not suppose, because it has been spoken concerning restoration, that ye shall be restored from sin to happiness. Behold, I say unto you, wickedness never was happiness.

11 And now, my son, all men that are in a state of nature, or I would say, in a carnal state, are in the gall of bitterness and in the bonds of iniquity; they are without God in the world, and they have gone contrary to the nature of God; therefore, they are in a state contrary to the nature of happiness.

12 And now behold, is the meaning of the word restoration to take a thing of a natural state and place it in an unnatural state, or to place it in a state opposite to its nature?

13 O, my son, this is not the case; but the meaning of the word restoration is to bring back again evil for evil, or carnal for carnal, or devilish for devilish—good for that which is good; righteous for that which is righteous; just for that which is just; merciful for that which is merciful.

14 Therefore, my son, see that you are merciful unto your brethren; deal justly, judge righteously, and do good continually; and if ye do all these things then shall ye receive your reward; yea, ye shall have mercy restored unto you again; ye shall have justice restored unto you again; ye shall have a righteous judgment restored unto you again; and ye shall have good rewarded unto you again.

15 For that which ye do send out shall return unto you again, and be restored; therefore, the word restoration more fully condemneth the sinner, and justifieth him not at all. (Alma 41)

If belief were sufficient to save, yet insufficient to magically change a sinner into a saint *during* this life, why should you assume that it could magically change a sinner into a saint *after* this life? Yet, this is exactly what proponents of "saved by belief" propose. Has God ever said that a sinner's tendency to sin magically disappears after death if they claimed to believe in him during life? Of course not.

If your religion does not have power to bring you into God's presence *now*, you have no reason to believe it will *then*. If it doesn't work now, it would be foolish to assume it will suddenly start working after you die.

This life is not a test to save those few who happen to encounter the gospel of Jesus and arbitrarily claim to believe in him. God is not arbitrary, and salvation is not so simple. If you truly desire salvation, the only way to obtain it is through complete surrender to God.

Born Again

*Marvel not that all mankind...must be born again...and
unless they do this, they can in nowise inherit the
kingdom of God. (Mosiah 27:25-26)*

The consequence of our individual sin is estrangement from God. The penalty of sin is not an arbitrary penalty from a vengeful God. Instead, it keeps us out of God's presence in this life, and causes us to permanently recoil from him in the hereafter.

> O, my beloved brethren, turn away from your sins; shake off the chains of him that would bind you fast; come unto that God who is the rock of your salvation. Prepare your souls for that glorious day when justice shall be administered unto the righteous, even the day of judgment, that ye may not shrink with awful fear; that ye may not remember your awful guilt in perfectness, and be constrained to exclaim: Holy, holy are thy judgments, O Lord God Almighty—but I know my guilt; I transgressed thy law, and my transgressions are mine; and the devil hath obtained me, that I am a prey to his awful misery. (2 Nephi 9:45-46)

If the penalty of sin were arbitrary, it would be arbitrarily simple to remove it. If sin's consequences were the result of an arbitrary decree from God, then an arbitrary decree from God could remove them. If this were the case, Jesus would not have had to condescend from heaven to be born on earth, he would not have had to live a perfect life, and would not have had to pay the price for our sins. Instead, he had to live a perfect life in a fallen world, finishing it with his bodily and spiritual sacrifice. His suffering in Gethsemane was so intense that "his sweat was as it were great drops of blood falling down to the ground" (Luke 22:44) He was whipped repeatedly, each lash bursting his flesh and muscle open. He had a crown of long thorns driven deep into his skin. He finished his sacrifice by hanging on a cross, suspended by large nails placed through his hands and feet. Truly, there is a consequence assigned for sin. Jesus illustrated this fact with the necessity of his suffering to pay the price of our sin.

The penalty of sin must be removed in order for us to dwell with God. This comes in two parts: First, we must be forgiven for past sins. Second, we must overcome those sins so as not to repeat them in the future.

Because of his sacrifice, Jesus Christ has been given power from his Father to forgive men of past sins: "And he hath power given unto him from the Father to redeem them from their sins because of repentance;" (Helaman 5:11) Whenever we sincerely ask for forgiveness, God forgives us. "If we confess our sins, he is faithful and just to forgive us our sins, and to cleanse us from all unrighteousness." (1 John 1:9)

Past sins, however, are not the only barrier to dwelling in God's presence in joy. If salvation simply required forgiveness of past sins, the state of being saved could not be much different than our current state. How could we imagine heaven to be a better place than earth if it is full of men and women with the same evil desires as those on earth?

To reconcile ourselves to God is not merely to ask for forgiveness, but to become the kind of person who would not transgress again. It requires a change in our character. If our desires are not aligned with God's, we are unclean before him.

> Wherefore, if ye have sought to do wickedly in the days of your probation, then ye are found unclean before the judgment-seat of God; and no unclean thing can dwell with God; wherefore, ye must be cast off forever. (1 Nephi 10:21)

Those whose desires are like God's desires will find that they also act like God. Being saved is much more than simply being forgiven. To be saved is to become like Christ. We must not only be forgiven of past sins, we must forsake them.

Forsaking past sin is not so easy, and usually not as quick as asking for forgiveness. However, abandonment is necessary:

Now my son, I would that ye should repent and forsake your sins...for except ye do this ye can in nowise inherit the kingdom of God. (Alma 39:9)

Through repentance, or changing our character to be like God's, we can return to God's presence. This is something we cannot do by ourselves, but it is also something that can't be done for us. Those who fully yield their desires and actions to God with a broken heart and a contrite spirit will not only be resurrected from the dead, but will find themselves able to endure God's presence, even before death.

This change in character is a process, not an event, but it begins with a single event. This event is known as entering the gate, being baptized with fire, having a mighty change of heart, or being born again. Like salvation itself, being born again is not a process that is only of our own making or only God's doing. Rather, it requires both parties.

What does it mean to be born again?

Jesus explained that to be born again does not mean to physically be reborn. Rather, it means to be born of water and spirit.

> 3 Jesus answered and said unto him, Verily, verily, I say unto thee, Except a man be born again, he cannot see the kingdom of God.
> 4 Nicodemus saith unto him, How can a man be born when he is old? can he enter the second time into his mother's womb, and be born?
> 5 Jesus answered, Verily, verily, I say unto thee, Except a man be born of water and of the Spirit, he cannot enter into the kingdom of God.
> 6 That which is born of the flesh is flesh; and that which is born of the Spirit is spirit. (John 3)

To be born of water is to repent and be baptized. This is the part of the process that is performed by the individual. Jesus said, "And again I say unto you, ye must repent, and be baptized in my name, and become as a little child, or ye can in nowise inherit the kingdom of God." (3 Nephi 11:38)

To be born of spirit is to be bathed in the Holy Ghost. This is the part of the process that is performed by God. Jesus said, "...after

41

that ye are baptized with water, behold, I will baptize you with fire and with the Holy Ghost;" (3 Nephi 12:1)

When one is born again, they—through a combination of personal repentance and an outpouring of God's power—enter into a state where they are redeemed from the fall of Adam, a state they continue in as long as they do not commit sin:

> 25 And the Lord said unto me: Marvel not that all mankind, yea, men and women, all nations, kindreds, tongues and people, must be born again; yea, born of God, changed from their carnal and fallen state, to a state of righteousness, being redeemed of God, becoming his sons and daughters;
> 26 And thus they become new creatures; and unless they do this, they can in nowise inherit the kingdom of God. (Mosiah 27)

Why is it necessary?

The goal of eternal life is possible only to those who have been born again. Living in heaven is only possible if you have been born again. Jesus said,

> Jesus answered, Verily, verily, I say unto thee, Except a man be born of water and of the Spirit, he cannot enter into the kingdom of God. (John 3:5)

One cannot be saved by themselves. By complying with the requirement of repentance, an individual qualifies for God to effect a change in their desires. Being washed in the Holy Spirit changes a person beyond what they can change of themselves. One group expressed it this way:

> "…the Spirit of the Lord Omnipotent, which has wrought a mighty change in us, or in our hearts, that we have no more disposition to do evil, but to do good continually." (Mosiah 5:2)

The mighty change in heart does not remove a person from the opposing temptation to do evil. Instead, it shifts the source of the disposition to do evil. Instead of coming from within, it comes from without.

The resulting purification allows increased communication with God through the Holy Spirit, enabling the individual instruction necessary to bring us to eternal life.

Being born again provides us with the confidence we need to stand in the presence of God:

> 14 And now behold, I ask of you, my brethren of the church, have ye spiritually been born of God? Have ye received his image in your countenances? Have ye experienced this mighty change in your hearts?
>
> 15 Do ye exercise faith in the redemption of him who created you? Do you look forward with an eye of faith, and view this mortal body raised in immortality, and this corruption raised in incorruption, to stand before God to be judged according to the deeds which have been done in the mortal body?
>
> 16 I say unto you, can you imagine to yourselves that ye hear the voice of the Lord, saying unto you, in that day: Come unto me ye blessed, for behold, your works have been the works of righteousness upon the face of the earth? (Alma 5)

Being born again is the launch pad from which we develop the ability to overcome all temptation and become sinless.

How does one become born again?

Becoming born again is simple, but it is not easy. The decision to turn to God is not one that should be taken lightly. One individual described his own experience as starting with an abrupt awareness of his sinful state and miserable destiny:

> 28 Nevertheless, after wading through much tribulation, *repenting nigh unto death*, the Lord in mercy hath seen fit to snatch me out of an everlasting burning, and I am born of God.
>
> 29 *My soul hath been redeemed* from the gall of bitterness and bonds of iniquity. I was in the darkest abyss; but

now I behold the marvelous light of God. My soul was racked with eternal torment; but I am snatched, and my soul is pained no more. (Mosiah 27)

Freedom from this bitterness can only come through total repentance. To repent is to reconcile oneself to God, or to bring one's actions, thoughts, and intentions into accordance with God's commandments. In other words, to submit to God in all things:

> For the natural man is an enemy to God, and has been from the fall of Adam, and will be, forever and ever, unless he yields to the enticings of the Holy Spirit, and putteth off the natural man and becometh a saint through the atonement of Christ the Lord, and becometh as a child, submissive, meek, humble, patient, full of love, willing to submit to all things which the Lord seeth fit to inflict upon him, even as a child doth submit to his father. (Mosiah 3:19)

Full submission to God is not an easy thing to achieve. Submission to God comes in phases. In the first phase, you seek to escape pain. This is what Paul referred to as the sorrow of the world.

> 9 Now I rejoice, not that ye were made sorry, but that ye sorrowed to repentance: for ye were made sorry after a godly manner, that ye might receive damage by us in nothing.
> 10 For godly sorrow worketh repentance to salvation not to be repented of: but the sorrow of the world worketh death. (2 Corinthians 7)

Worldly sorrow is not sufficient to save. Those with worldly sorrow ask God to relieve their pain. Whether he does or not, they rarely change.

Worldly sorrow is simply the misery of the damned. It is misery caused by a difference between one's reality and one's lustful desires. There may be depression, bitterness, despair, or sorrow, but without seeking God's will.

In phase two, you experience godly sorrow. Godly sorrow is the realization that the emptiness and darkness within your heart is the result of rebellion against God. You realize that you have become desensitized and that you have preferred darkness to light, your own will to Christ's. The sorrow you feel comes not from the temporal consequences of your sin, but from your awareness of your offense to God. It causes you to change. It creates a desire to move forward in submission to God.

The next phase of submission is initial sacrifice. In this stage, you are willing to make limited changes to your life to move towards God. This degree of sacrifice is portrayed in the scriptures when kings willingly offer up "half their kingdom" to satisfy the requests of a person they seek to appease (see Esther 5:6, Alma 20:23, etc.). Here, you remove things from your life that offend God, and start doing the things he has commanded you to do.

The next phase is full sacrifice. In this phase, you remove all boundaries on what you are willing to give God in order to appease him.

> O God, Aaron hath told me that there is a God; and if there is a God, and if thou art God, wilt thou make thyself known unto me, and I will give away *all* my sins to know thee, and that I may be raised from the dead, and be saved at the last day. And now when the king had said these words, he was struck as if he were dead. (Alma 22:18)

It is only in this last phase that an individual has achieved full submission. They are not seeking their own lives, their own comfort, or to retain or restore any worldly attainment in their lives. They have an eye single to the glory of God, and their only desire is to please God. This is the sacrifice that God requires. This is full submission.

Another way full submission is described is with the phrase "broken heart and contrite spirit":

> And ye shall offer for a sacrifice unto me a broken heart and a contrite spirit. And whoso cometh unto me with a broken heart and a contrite spirit, him will I baptize with fire and with the Holy Ghost... (3 Nephi 9:20)

A broken heart and contrite spirit is when your desire to obey God becomes so great that it crushes any other desire in your life. A broken heart and contrite spirit is what, through the sacrifice of Jesus Christ, qualifies you for eternal life:

6 Wherefore, redemption cometh in and through the Holy Messiah; for he is full of grace and truth.

7 Behold, he offereth himself a sacrifice for sin, to answer the ends of the law, unto all those who have a broken heart and a contrite spirit; and unto none else can the ends of the law be answered.

8 Wherefore, how great the importance to make these things known unto the inhabitants of the earth, that they may know that there is no flesh that can dwell in the presence of God, save it be through the merits, and mercy, and grace of the Holy Messiah, who layeth down his life according to the flesh, and taketh it again by the power of the Spirit, that he may bring to pass the resurrection of the dead, being the first that should rise. (2 Nephi 2)

Most people are blissfully ignorant of their true standing with God. Either they don't believe in him, or they fool themselves into thinking that their religion has reconciled them to him when such is not the case. Typically, a broken heart and contrite spirit can only occur in an individual who understands his true situation with God due to the fall, and what awaits him if he meets God without preparing for the event. For example, this is how one minister helped a powerful king to achieve a broken heart and contrite spirit through understanding the fall, the mission of Christ, and the need for personal repentance:

13 And Aaron did expound unto him the scriptures from the creation of Adam, laying the fall of man before him, and their carnal state and also the plan of redemption, which was prepared from the foundation of the world, through Christ, for all whosoever would believe on his name.

14 And since man had fallen he could not merit anything of himself; but the sufferings and death of Christ atone for their sins, through faith and repentance, and so forth; and that he breaketh the bands of death, that the grave shall have no victory, and that the sting of death should be swallowed up in the hopes of glory; and Aaron did expound all these things unto the king.

15 And it came to pass that after Aaron had expounded these things unto him, the king said: What shall I do that I may have this eternal life of which thou hast spoken? Yea, what shall I do that I may be born of God, having this wicked spirit rooted out of my breast, and receive his Spirit, that I may be filled with joy, that I may not be cast off at the last day? Behold, said he, I will give up all that I possess, yea, I will forsake my kingdom, that I may receive this great joy.

16 But Aaron said unto him: If thou desirest this thing, if thou wilt bow down before God, yea, *if thou wilt repent of all thy sins*, and will bow down before God, and call on his name in faith, believing that ye shall receive, then shalt thou receive the hope which thou desirest.

17 And it came to pass that when Aaron had said these words, the king did bow down before the Lord, upon his knees; yea, even he did prostrate himself upon the earth, and cried mightily, saying:

18 O God, Aaron hath told me that there is a God; and if there is a God, and if thou art God, wilt thou make thyself known unto me, and *I will give away all my sins to know thee*, and that I may be raised from the dead, and be saved at the last day… (Alma 22)

Turning away from our sins is not complete without baptism by immersion in water, a rite prescribed by God through which an individual can signal to God that he has made the decision to turn to him without reservation.

14 Now I say unto you that ye must repent, and be *born again*; for the Spirit saith if ye are not born again ye cannot inherit the kingdom of heaven; therefore come and *be baptized unto repentance*, that ye may be washed from your sins, that ye may have faith on the Lamb of God, who taketh away the sins of the world, who is mighty to save and to cleanse from all unrighteousness.

15 Yea, I say unto you come and fear not, and *lay aside every sin*, which easily doth beset you, which doth bind you down to destruction, yea, come and go forth, and *show unto your God that ye are willing to repent of your sins* and

47

enter into a covenant with him to keep his commandments, and witness it unto him this day by going into the waters of baptism. (Alma 7)

And he commandeth all men that they must repent, and be baptized in his name, having perfect faith in the Holy One of Israel, or they cannot be saved in the kingdom of God. (2 Nephi 9:23)

To the apostles of the New Testament, Jesus gave authority to baptize those who repented: "Go ye therefore, and teach all nations, baptizing them in the name of the Father, and of the Son, and of the Holy Ghost:" (Matthew 28:19) He did the same to his believers on this continent when he visited here after his resurrection: "I give unto you power that ye shall baptize this people when I am again ascended into heaven." (3 Nephi 11:21)

To ensure that baptism is an effectual promise made with God, it ought to be done according to the terms he has set. A person should be taught what it means to repent, should repent of all their sins, be completely committed to keeping all his commandments throughout their life, and should be baptized by immersion by someone following the instructions the Lord has given:

23 Verily I say unto you, that whoso repenteth of his sins through your words, and desireth to be baptized in my name, on this wise shall ye baptize them—Behold, ye shall go down and stand in the water, and in my name shall ye baptize them.
24 And now behold, these are the words which ye shall say, calling them by name, saying:
25 Having authority given me of Jesus Christ, I baptize you in the name of the Father, and of the Son, and of the Holy Ghost. Amen.
26 And then shall ye immerse them in the water, and come forth again out of the water.
27 And after this manner shall ye baptize in my name; for behold, verily I say unto you, that the Father, and the Son, and the Holy Ghost are one; and I am in the Father, and the Father in me, and the Father and I are one.

28 And according as I have commanded you thus shall ye baptize. (3 Nephi 11)

Those performing the baptism ought to qualify for baptism themselves by having completely repented of their sins and feel comfortable declaring that they have "authority given [them] of Jesus Christ."

Any other form of baptism, though it might have value for the participants, will fall short of the attendant blessings of a true baptism in the way the Lord has directed.

The beginning, not the end

The mighty change that occurs with baptism by fire is neither permanent nor unconditional. It lasts as long as the conditions of repentance are maintained.

> And whosoever doeth this, *and keepeth the commandments of God from thenceforth,* the same will remember that I say unto him, yea, he will remember that I have said unto him, he shall have eternal life, according to the testimony of the Holy Spirit, which testifieth in me. (Alma 7:16)

Maintaining this condition is called retaining a remission of your sins.

A remission of your sins can be retained as long as you maintain a broken heart and a contrite spirit. In other words, as long as you continue to hunger and thirst for God's word, and you submit to it and live it as soon as you receive it, you will remain in the same state you entered into upon being born again.

Being born again is the first event in a process leading to eternal life, and not the culmination of obtaining eternal life. It is described in the scriptures as "entering the gate" or "starting on the path" to eternal life.

> 17 Wherefore, do the things which I have told you I have seen that your Lord and your Redeemer should do; for, for this cause have they been shown unto me, that ye might know the gate by which ye should enter. For the gate by which ye should enter is repentance and baptism

by water; and then cometh a remission of your sins by fire and by the Holy Ghost.

18 And then are ye in this strait and narrow path which leads to eternal life; yea, ye have entered in by the gate; ye have done according to the commandments of the Father and the Son; and ye have received the Holy Ghost, which witnesses of the Father and the Son, unto the fulfilling of the promise which he hath made, that if ye entered in by the way ye should receive.

19 And now, my beloved brethren, after ye have gotten into this strait and narrow path, I would ask if all is done? Behold, I say unto you, Nay; for ye have not come thus far save it were by the word of Christ with unshaken faith in him, relying wholly upon the merits of him who is mighty to save.

20 Wherefore, ye must press forward with a steadfastness in Christ, having a perfect brightness of hope, and a love of God and of all men. Wherefore, if ye shall press forward, feasting upon the word of Christ, and endure to the end, behold, thus saith the Father: Ye shall have eternal life. (2 Nephi 31:17)

A person who is on the path to eternal life retains a remission of sins by keeping God's commandments.

We know that whosoever is born of God sinneth not; but he that is begotten of God keepeth himself, and that wicked one toucheth him not. (1 John 5:18. See also 1 John 3:1-10)

When someone who has been born again sins, they remove themselves from the path to eternal life. They have failed to "endure to the end":

And if they will not repent and believe in his name, and be baptized in his name, and endure to the end, they must be damned; for the Lord God, the Holy One of Israel, has spoken it. (2 Nephi 9:24)

Those who have left the path can reenter it the same way they did before: by entering in at the gate, or fully repenting of their sins, fully submitting to God, and being born again.

The sacrifice of Jesus Christ provides us with a way to be forgiven of the sins we have committed, submit to him fully, and receive a spiritual rebirth. After being reborn, we are given the rest of our lives to follow Jesus by living his commandments. Our lives become a probation, to test us to see if we will keep God's commandments. "… there was a space granted unto man in which he might repent; therefore this life became a probationary state; a time to prepare to meet God…" (Alma 12:24) If we do, we will qualify to live with him. If we do not, we must repent and begin to live his commandments, or we will continue disqualifying ourselves from dwelling with him.

Crucify the Flesh

Yea doubtless, and I count all things but loss for the excellency of the knowledge of Christ Jesus my Lord: for whom I have suffered the loss of all things, and do count them but dung, that I may win Christ. (Philippians 3:8)

A full relationship with God requires the surrender of all things. This stout principle is stated plainly over and over again in scripture. Few encounter a full relationship with God, because few understand or submit fully in surrender to God.

There are three levels of surrender to God. The first is partial surrender, when you are willing to surrender a specific thing or a group of specific things. Many people in this group are honest enough to recognize that their unsurrendered things should be surrendered, but they love those things too much to let go of them. Their unwillingness to let go of these things in spite of a commandment from God to do so means that they love these things more than God, which is a violation of the first and great commandment: Love God with all your heart (see Matthew 22:38). Their withholdings are an idol to them, and as long as they hold onto these unsurrendered things, they cannot have a full relationship with God. No matter what positive experiences they have with God, they will be forever blocked from the much greater portion they were meant to experience.

Some less honest people in this group think that their unsurrendered list is acceptable to God because it is comprised only of things they think God will never expect them to surrender. Who are you to dictate what is right and what is wrong to God? If your operating assumption is that you are fallen and incapable of saving yourself, how could you ever think that you are capable of dictating what God can and can't do? God's humbling interchange with Job fits any who think for a moment that their wisdom exceeds God's (see Job 38). The Lord's ways are higher than yours:

> 8 For my thoughts are not your thoughts, neither are your ways my ways, saith the Lord.
> 9 For as the heavens are higher than the earth, so are my ways higher than your ways, and my thoughts than your thoughts. (Isaiah 55:8-9)

When it comes to what God might ask of us, there are no limitations. Abraham probably thought God would never ask him to sacrifice a human, let alone his son, let alone the son whose life was required to fulfill promises he had received from God. And yet, he did not withhold Isaac. There are many other examples in the scriptures. Nothing is out of bounds. Even your relationship with your parents and your children are among what he can ask you to sacrifice:

> He that loveth father or mother more than me is not worthy of me: and he that loveth son or daughter more than me is not worthy of me. (Matthew 10:37)

> If any [man] come to me, and hate not his father, and mother, and wife, and children, and brethren, and sisters, yea, and his own life also, he cannot be my disciple. (Luke 14:26)

Sacrifice is something that God can ask of you over anything, at any time. He described this as taking up your cross. It is required, and is required daily:

> And whosoever doth not bear his cross, and come after me, cannot be my disciple. (Luke 14:27)

> And he said to them all, If any man will come after me, let him deny himself, and take up his cross daily, and follow me. (Luke 9:23)

Ironically, those who put God in a box do so out of fear. They fear that if they let God out of their boxes, he would end up less loving, less merciful, or less good than they presently imagine him to be. That is ironic because it is only by removing your limitations of him that you can see just how loving, merciful, and good he really is. Trusting him provides the opportunity for him to prove his faithfulness and love. It far exceeds anything you can imagine when you box him up in false traditions. If you look at every person in the scriptures who came to know God, you will struggle to find someone who found him less godly upon getting to know him. Instead, you see the opposite. You see deep, loving, worshipful reverence increase in proportion to how well someone knows God.

Putting God in a box does not protect you from disappointment. Anytime we impede God's will in our lives, we willingly limit the amount of love he can show to us. You may have experienced God in some way—spiritual gifts, revelation, joy, or even visitations— but your experiences are limited and diminished compared to what he could give you if you would unconditionally trust in him.

In the scriptures, there are those who had miracles, those who had revelation, those that experienced great joy, those that saw him, even those that touched him. But of those who experienced God in some way, how many were able to abide in his glory? The answer is surprisingly few. With almost every experience, he held something back, sometimes considerably so. Every commandment you refuse to consider diminishes your potential glory, but it also diminishes the quantity of the Lord's glory you are able to abide. For each thing "your God would never ask you to do," you remove yourself from the opportunity to experience that much more of him.

Instead of seeing a potential sacrifice as off limits to God, you should recognize that thing as the limit of your trust in God. Focusing on these limits in this perspective outlines where you need to change rather than demarcating how far you will go in your relationship with God. You should repent, and come to the point where you are willing to put everything on the altar.

God has never given you a reason to doubt him. In all his interactions, he has faithfully honored your trust in him. Why hesitate to give him whatever he asks? He loves you and will never ask of you what is not in your best interest to give.

When you choose to lay aside what you think you know about God, and instead ask him about the things you fear, he will take away your fear by revealing to you a greater depth of his love, perfection, mercy, and glory than you have ever comprehended. With each revelation, your trust in him will increase until it is unshakeable.

Perfect love removes all fear. If you truly love God, then seek to know him on his terms, holding nothing back. Only those who put everything they think they know about God on the altar can come to know him.

The second level of surrender is surrender in all things that you know of. This is the category all Christians should strive to reside in. This is where you can say with an honest heart that you have complied with every request God has made of you. This is the place you need to be in order to experience a more significant relationship with God than what is available to those who hold back. Yet, even in this category, you have not achieved a full relationship with God. As you progress with God in this category, he will show you things you have not previously considered, and you will realize that you still have corners of your heart that you have not surrendered to him.

A wonderful example of this principle is given by the interaction of a rich young man with the Lord Jesus:

> 17 And when he was gone forth into the way, there came one running, and kneeled to him, and asked him, Good Master, what shall I do that I may inherit eternal life?
> 18 And Jesus said unto him, Why callest thou me good? there is none good but one, that is, God.
> 19 Thou knowest the commandments, Do not commit adultery, Do not kill, Do not steal, Do not bear false witness, Defraud not, Honour thy father and mother.
> 20 And he answered and said unto him, Master, all these have I observed from my youth.
> 21 Then Jesus beholding him loved him, and said unto him, One thing thou lackest: go thy way, sell whatsoever thou hast, and give to the poor, and thou shalt have treasure in heaven: and come, take up the cross, and follow me.
> 22 And he was sad at that saying, and went away grieved: for he had great possessions. (Mark 10)

The rich young ruler *thought* he had sacrificed everything, but he hadn't. Jesus helped him see what more he had to do. There were more commandments that he was not yet aware of. We also think we are done far before we actually are. You aren't there until you are actually there, and if you quit, you'll never experience the promised blessings.

55

Those who approach God can count on receiving new commandments. They can count on being asked to sacrifice in ways they did not expect. If they already knew and did everything that was required, they would already possess the relationship they seek.

Be prepared for paradigm shifts. In order to take us higher, God has to rip out our foundations. He purges every branch before it can bear more fruit:

> 1 I am the true vine, and my Father is the husbandman. 2 Every branch in me that beareth not fruit he taketh away: and every branch that beareth fruit, he purgeth it, that it may bring forth more fruit. (John 15)

God will teach and call to further repentance everyone who comes to him. That is his mission, to bring men higher than they are.

What is called the "Abrahamic sacrifice" is actually not one sacrifice, but many successive sacrifices that come one after another as we obey what God asks at any given time. Abraham's sacrifice of Isaac was critical, but it wasn't the first time Abraham was tried. Abraham was tried as a child when he was assigned to guard his idol-maker father's wares and chose to destroy them. He was tried when exposed to textual accounts of Shem, Noah, and the fathers and their experiences with God. He recognized that his father's religion was inferior, and chose to believe there was something better. He was tried when he endured his father's hand among those who sought to sacrifice him, and tried when he had the opportunity to forgive him. He was tried when commanded to leave his home in Ur. He was tried when his father and brother—whom he had rescued through his own merits and mercy—turned away from him. He was tried when his wife was taken by a rich and powerful ruler—twice—for long periods of time without his knowledge of her condition or any likelihood that she would come back to him. He was tried when he took Hagar to wife. He was tried when his marriages were ravaged by the jealousy of Sarah. He was tried when God told him that his beloved son Ishmael would not be his heir. He was tried when Lot, whom he had sacrificed so much for, selfishly chose the better section of land at their parting, revealing Lot's persisting weaknesses in spite of Abraham's sacrifices on his behalf. He was tried when he went into battle to rescue Lot. He was tried when he parted ways with Ishmael and Hagar. And finally, he was tried when he was asked to sacrifice Isaac.

Sacrifice is not an event, but a process. While it almost always includes giving something up, it frequently includes taking on something new. These things are not always material objects. They frequently include letting go of treasured traditions or taking on new beliefs. The goal of that process is to successively increase your trust in God until you are willing to yield completely to him without exception—the third level of surrender.

The third level of surrender is surrender in all things known and unknown. This is the point we must reach to have the full relationship with God that he intended for us. In this stage, your trust for God is so great that you would do anything he might command, no matter what it is, and there is nothing that you would not do if he commanded it. At this point, your obedience to him is not a function of your experience or knowledge. No matter what he reveals to you, you will obey. Whereas level two is a case-by-case basis, dependent on the specific sacrifice, level three is total.

Surrender of all things is described by Paul as being crucified in the flesh: "And they that are Christ's have crucified the flesh with the affections and lusts." (Galatians 5:24) The person who reaches this point has subdued all their desires to God's will.

The Lord described total submission as equivalent to losing one's life: "He that findeth his life shall lose it: and he that loseth his life for my sake shall find it." (Matthew 10:39) He showed this type of submission in his own life. Crucifixion is not temporary or by degrees. It is total. When you lose your life, you are not merely setting aside a part of it.

Crucifying the flesh has an enormous cost, but it also provides an uncountable blessing. When you give everything, you get everything. You can't inherit the glory of the ancients without making the same degree of sacrifice of the ancients. When you make the same degree of sacrifice as the ancients, God—who is no respecter of persons—will reward you with the same experiences as the ancients. Those who are willing to lose their life will save it, or receive full communion with God:

> Verily, verily, I say unto you, Except a corn of wheat fall into the ground and die, it abideth alone: but if it die, it bringeth forth much fruit. (John 12:24)

When we reach this point, we have lost our lives because we no longer live for ourselves, but for God:

I am crucified with Christ: nevertheless I live; yet not I, but Christ liveth in me: and the life which I now live in the flesh I live by the faith of the Son of God, who loved me, and gave himself for me. (Galatians 2:20)

The cost is incredible. It is total. Realizing this is an important distinction between the second and third levels of sacrifice:

> 28 For which of you, intending to build a tower, sitteth not down first, and counteth the cost, whether he have sufficient to finish it?
> 29 Lest haply, after he hath laid the foundation, and is not able to finish it, all that behold it begin to mock him,
> 30 Saying, This man began to build, and was not able to finish.
> 31 Or what king, going to make war against another king, sitteth not down first, and consulteth whether he be able with ten thousand to meet him that cometh against him with twenty thousand?
> 32 Or else, while the other is yet a great way off, he sendeth an ambassage, and desireth conditions of peace.
> 33 So likewise, whosoever he be of you that forsaketh not all that he hath, he cannot be my disciple. (Luke 14)

Real sacrifice is a response to God's requests. It is not simply inventing things that make our lives more difficult. We cannot live through God while still pursuing our own agenda, even if that agenda causes personal suffering. Sacrifices that we invent are not from God. Cain invented a sacrifice and despite it being similar to the sacrifice God ordained, it was rejected by God (see Genesis 4:4-5). Saul performed the same sacrifice as Samuel, but it was rejected by God (see 1 Samuel 13). In both cases, there were extreme consequences for their offering sacrifices that were not requested from God:

> And Samuel said, Hath the LORD as great delight in burnt offerings and sacrifices, as in obeying the voice of the LORD? Behold, to obey is better than sacrifice, and to hearken than the fat of rams. (1 Samuel 15:22)

Do not succumb to the temptation to invent ways to punish yourself in order to distract you from the real sacrifice God is asking of you. If you do, you will either find yourself without the progress you could have by focusing on God, or you will find yourself retrograding when your sacrifice does not result in any spiritual progress. God's path is hard enough—you don't have to invent things to make it more difficult. Instead, use that energy to ask him what he wants you to do, and do it.

A full relationship with God requires full trust in God. You can't hold anything back. God will require of you anything you haven't already given him. It is total submission no matter what God may ask of you. Submission is a perishable status. We must die daily to the Lord!

Be Ye Perfect

Therefore I would that ye should be perfect even as I, or your Father who is in heaven is perfect. (3 Nephi 12:48)

The presence of the Lord causes the earth to tremble. The Psalmist wrote, "tremble, thou earth, at the presence of the Lord, at the presence of the God of Jacob;" (Psalm 114:7) "The earth shook, the heavens also dropped at the presence of God: even Sinai itself was moved at the presence of God, the God of Israel." (Psalm 68:8)

The presence of God is a consuming fire. "The Lord thy God is a consuming fire, even a jealous God." (Deuteronomy 4:24). The wicked are tormented by fire in his presence. The Psalmist wrote that "As smoke is driven away, so drive them away: as wax melteth before the fire, so let the wicked perish at the presence of God." (Psalm 68:2) John said:

> The same shall drink of the wine of the wrath of God, which is poured out without mixture into the cup of his indignation; and he shall be tormented with fire and brimstone in the presence of the holy angels, and in the presence of the Lamb: (Revelation 14:10)

His presence consumes everything that is corruptible:

> A fire goeth before him, and burneth up his enemies round about. His lightnings enlightened the world: the earth saw, and trembled. The hills melted like wax at the presence of the Lord, at the presence of the Lord of the whole earth. (Psalm 97:3-5)

What endures before God's presence? What remains after refinement? What endures through the fire?

> But who may abide the day of his coming, and who shall stand when he appeareth? For he is like a refiner's fire, and like fuller's soap. And he shall sit as a refiner and purifier of silver; and he shall purify the sons of Levi, and purge them as gold and silver, that they may offer unto the Lord an offering in righteousness. (3 Nephi 24:2-3)

Those who are pure will withstand the presence of God. When we "shall have a perfect knowledge of all our guilt, and our uncleanness, and our nakedness" it will be "the righteous [who] shall have a perfect knowledge of their enjoyment, and their righteousness, being clothed with purity, yea, even with the robe of righteousness." (2 Nephi 9:13-14) It is **only** those who are clothed upon with purity—those who have reconciled themselves to God's commandments—that can dwell in God's presence.

> And he hath brought to pass the redemption of the world, whereby he that is found guiltless before him at the judgment day hath it given unto him to dwell in the presence of God in his kingdom, to sing ceaseless praises with the choirs above, unto the Father, and unto the Son, and unto the Holy Ghost, which are one God, in a state of happiness which hath no end. (Mormon 7:7)

God does not tolerate even the least degree of sin.

The idea that a man can be a sinner and still dwell in God's presence is a fabrication created by men. If you are in violation of the commandments of God, as far as you know them, to any degree, you are not guiltless before God. The only way you can be guiltless before God is to be reconciled to God's commandments.

We must avoid the temptation to excuse ourselves for our sins:

> 7 Yea, and there shall be many which shall say: Eat, drink, and be merry, for tomorrow we die; and it shall be well with us.

8 And there shall also be many which shall say: Eat, drink, and be merry; nevertheless, fear God—he will justify in committing a little sin; yea, lie a little, take the advantage of one because of his words, dig a pit for thy neighbor; there is no harm in this; and do all these things, for tomorrow we die; and if it so be that we are guilty, God will beat us with a few stripes, and at last we shall be saved in the kingdom of God.

9 Yea, and there shall be many which shall teach after this manner, false and vain and foolish doctrines...

11 Yea, they have all gone out of the way; they have become corrupted.

14 ...they have all gone astray save it be a few, who are the humble followers of Christ; nevertheless, they are led, that in many instances they do err because they are taught by the precepts of men.

15 O the wise, and the learned, and the rich, that are puffed up in the pride of their hearts, and all those who preach false doctrines, and all those who commit whoredoms, and pervert the right way of the Lord, wo, wo, wo be unto them, saith the Lord God Almighty, for they shall be thrust down to hell! (2 Nephi 28)

Those who believe that God can tolerate sin in the least degree ignore his word; "the Lord cannot look upon sin with the least degree of allowance." (Alma 45:16) Those who knowingly engage in sin are cut off from God's presence. Even partial sin leads to complete condemnation, according to God's word.

Therefore, thou son of man, say unto the children of thy people, The righteousness of the righteous shall not deliver him in the day of his transgression: as for the wickedness of the wicked, he shall not fall thereby in the day that he turneth from his wickedness; neither shall the righteous be able to live for his righteousness in the day that he sinneth. (Ezekiel 33:12)

God cannot save sinners *in* their sins. He can only save sinners *from* their sins.

34 And Zeezrom said again: Shall he save his people in their sins? And Amulek answered and said unto him: I say unto you he shall not, for it is impossible for him to deny his word.

35 Now Zeezrom said unto the people: See that ye remember these things; for he said there is but one God; yet he saith that the Son of God shall come, but he shall not save his people—as though he had authority to command God. (Alma 11:34-35)

Salvation is not about sinning *less*. It is about not sinning *at all*. This is a bold and extreme statement, but analysis of scripture will bear it out.

It is possible to become sinless in this life.

Is it possible to keep all of God's commandments? If you don't think so, chances are you have adopted a theology where God permits at least some sin. Man's failure, not God's word, is the source of that false doctrine.

Only those who believe it is possible will ever try. In order to become sinless, it requires faith in God. It is impossible to exercise God's power without faith, and it is impossible to have faith in a principle that you do not believe *could* be true. In order to describe how to become sinless, we must first show that it is possible.

That the goal of the gospel is to produce sinless men is undeniable. Paul described his mission as perfecting every man in Christ Jesus:

Whom we preach, warning every man, and teaching every man in all wisdom; that we may present every man perfect in Christ Jesus: (Colossians 1:28)

In another letter, he clarified that "perfect in Christ" meant to achieve a stature similar to that of Jesus:

Till we all come in the unity of the faith, and of the knowledge of the Son of God, unto a perfect man, unto the measure of the stature of the fulness of Christ: (Ephesians 4:13)

Mormon described the possibility of being found spotless at the great and last day:

> O then ye unbelieving, turn ye unto the Lord; cry mightily unto the Father in the name of Jesus, that perhaps *ye may be found spotless*, pure, fair, and white, having been cleansed by the blood of the Lamb, at that great and last day. (Mormon 9:6)

John the Revelator described true disciples of God as those who purify themselves, becoming like Jesus by not sinning and keeping Jesus' commandments:

> 1 Behold, what manner of love the Father hath bestowed upon us, that we should be called the sons of God: therefore the world knoweth us not, because it knew him not.
>
> 2 Beloved, now are we the sons of God, and it doth not yet appear what we shall be: but we know that, when he shall appear, we shall be like him; for we shall see him as he is.
>
> 3 And every man that hath this hope in him purifieth himself, even as he is pure.
>
> 4 Whosoever committeth sin transgresseth also the law: for sin is the transgression of the law.
>
> 5 And ye know that he was manifested to take away our sins; and in him is no sin.
>
> 6 Whosoever abideth in him sinneth not: whosoever sinneth hath not seen him, neither known him.
>
> 7 Little children, let no man deceive you: he that doeth righteousness is righteous, even as he is righteous.
>
> 8 *He that committeth sin is of the devil;* for the devil sinneth from the beginning. For this purpose the Son of God was manifested, that he might destroy the works of the devil.
>
> 9 *Whosoever is born of God doth not commit sin;* for his seed remaineth in him: and he cannot sin, because he is born of God.
>
> 10 In this the children of God are manifest, and the children of the devil: whosoever doeth not righteousness

is not of God, neither he that loveth not his brother. (1 John 3)

Jesus, our example in all things, lived a sinless life. One of the reasons Jesus had to come to this earth as a man is to prove that it is within the capacity of man to perfectly obey God. If it were not so, God could not justly require full obedience to him.

It *is* possible to become free from sin:

> ...that ye may become the sons of God; that when he shall appear we shall be like him, for we shall see him as he is; that we may have this hope; that we may be purified even as he is pure. Amen. (Moroni 7:48)

It is also essential.

People who are capable of sin cannot live with God.

The Lord makes it clear that those who fail to keep his commandments cannot endure his presence:

> Now my son, I would that ye should repent and forsake your sins...for except ye do this ye can in nowise inherit the kingdom of God. (Alma 39:9)

> ...inasmuch as ye will not keep the commandments of God ye shall be cut off from his presence. (Alma 38:1)

> ...the Lord cannot look upon sin with the least degree of allowance. (Alma 45:16)

> [Those who] obey not the gospel of our Lord Jesus Christ...shall be punished with everlasting destruction from the presence of the Lord, and from the glory of his power... (2 Thessalonians 1:8-9)

Many mistakenly think that all that is required to dwell with God is to be forgiven of one's sins. Forgiveness of sins covers past transgression, but does not change who you are. One who is capable of sin remains capable of sin despite having been forgiven of past sin.

21 And if the Lord shall say—Because of thine iniquities thou shalt be cut off from my presence—he will cause that it shall be so.

22 And wo unto him to whom he shall say this, for it shall be unto him *that will* do iniquity, and he cannot be saved; therefore, for this cause, that men might be saved, hath repentance been declared. (Helaman 12)

Those who will continue in sin—even if forgiven of past sin—cannot dwell with God.

But the fearful, and unbelieving, and the abominable, and murderers, and whoremongers, and sorcerers, and idolaters, and all liars, shall have their part in the lake which burneth with fire and brimstone: which is the second death. (Revelation 21:8)

Jesus can temporarily admit us into his presence by forgiving us of our past sins. For example, Isaiah recoiled from God's presence until he was told that his sins had been forgiven:

Woe is me! for I am undone; because I am a man of unclean lips, and I dwell in the midst of a people of unclean lips: for mine eyes have seen the King, the Lord of hosts. (Isaiah 6:5)

However, the indescribable pain felt by those with unforgiven sin will return to such a one as soon as they sin again.

An individual capable of sin cannot dwell permanently in the presence of God, because he will soon sin again, causing him to recoil from the presence of God due to the indescribable pain of enduring his presence while in sin.

Perfect in Christ

While we are wrong to assume it is not possible to obey all of God's commandments, we are right to recognize that Jesus was greater than any man who has lived or will live on this earth. We ought not compare ourselves to Jesus in the sense of his knowledge or power.

However, we can—and are commanded to—duplicate his desire for good and perfect obedience to God.

We can be perfect as Jesus is perfect without being equal to him. This seemingly paradoxical position makes sense when one realizes that God gives different commandments to different people at different times according to their capacity. To be perfect in Christ, you must simply obey every commandment you have received from God. This is not the same as obeying all the commandments he has given to others. For example, the commandment you receive from God will differ from those that the Lord received from his Father. Because he was further advanced than any other mortal, he was given commandments harder to obey than any other mortal.

God has promised that we will never be commanded beyond our capacity to obey.

> And it came to pass that I, Nephi, said unto my father: I will go and do the things which the Lord hath commanded, for I know that the Lord giveth no commandments unto the children of men, save he shall prepare a way for them that they may accomplish the thing which he commandeth them. (1 Nephi 3:7)

> There hath no temptation taken you but such as is common to man: but God is faithful, who will not suffer you to be tempted above that ye are able; but will with the temptation also make a way to escape, that ye may be able to bear it. (1 Corinthians 10:13)

We can be confident that any commandment of which we are aware is within our capacity to obey. That is a profound truth that ought to lead to significant change in your life. You can move forward with the confidence that any trial you face has been given to you by a loving God with full confidence of your capacity to obey.

As you grow in ability, God will reveal more and different commandments to you. To be perfect in Christ is to maintain obedience to all commandments that you know. It is to be reconciled to the portion of God's word of which you are aware.

> 32 Yea, come unto Christ, and be perfected in him, and deny yourselves of all ungodliness; and if ye shall deny

yourselves of all ungodliness, and love God with all your might, mind and strength, then is his grace sufficient for you, that by his grace ye may be perfect in Christ; and if by the grace of God ye are perfect in Christ, ye can in nowise deny the power of God.

33 And again, if ye by the grace of God are perfect in Christ, and deny not his power, then are ye sanctified in Christ by the grace of God, through the shedding of the blood of Christ, which is in the covenant of the Father unto the remission of your sins, that ye become holy, without spot. (Moroni 10)

The path to salvation, then, is to first repent, and then to keep God's commandments with perfect obedience as they are revealed to you.

3 And it is requisite with the justice of God that men should be judged according to their works; and if their works were good in this life, and the desires of their hearts were good, that they should also, at the last day, be restored unto that which is good.

4 And if their works are evil they shall be restored unto them for evil. Therefore, all things shall be restored to their proper order, every thing to its natural frame—mortality raised to immortality, corruption to incorruption—raised to endless happiness to inherit the kingdom of God, or to endless misery to inherit the kingdom of the devil, the one on one hand, the other on the other—

5 The one raised to happiness according to his desires of happiness, or good according to his desires of good; and the other to evil according to his desires of evil; for as he has desired to do evil all the day long even so shall he have his reward of evil when the night cometh.

6 And so it is on the other hand. *If he hath repented of his sins,* **and** *desired righteousness until the end of his days,* even so he shall be rewarded unto righteousness. (Alma 41)

The standard commandments found in the scriptures provide a starting point. If you want to draw closer to God, read the scriptures prayerfully and identify each commandment you are currently disobeying. Repent and fulfill the commandments. God will also give you individual commandments. These can resemble scriptural commandments in scope and form, or could be one-time instructions. Custom commandments can range from mundane to deeply profound. No matter how arbitrary it may seem, it is of utmost importance to keep any commandment God gives you or has given you, including what is contained in the scriptures.

As you obey what God has revealed, he will reveal more to you, which you are likewise obligated to obey. If you continue faithful, he will reveal more to you. God will increase the difficulty of each commandment to correspond with your increasing spiritual strength. Eventually, he will reveal to you all the laws that you need to live to be comfortable in his presence.

If we keep God's commandments without fail, we will be able to bear his presence.

> 21 Dear friends, if we feel at ease in the presence of God, we will have the courage to come near him.
> 22 He will give us whatever we ask, because we obey him and do what pleases him. (1 John 3, CEV)

There is no other way.

Righteous desire, even unto death

Because God has promised that he will never give you a commandment that you do not have the capacity to obey, you can rest assured that the one and only reason for your disobedience is a lack of desire.

We are given everything necessary to become saved. If we fail in the task after having been correctly instructed in the gospel, it can only be for lack of desire.

> 27 Wherefore, men are free according to the flesh; and all things are given them which are expedient unto man. And they are free to choose liberty and eternal life, through the great Mediator of all men, or to choose captivity and death, according to the captivity and power

69

of the devil; for he seeketh that all men might be miserable like unto himself.

28 And now, my sons, I would that ye should look to the great Mediator, and hearken unto his great commandments; and be faithful unto his words, and choose eternal life, according to the will of his Holy Spirit;

29 And not choose eternal death, according to the will of the flesh and the evil which is therein, which giveth the spirit of the devil power to captivate, to bring you down to hell, that he may reign over you in his own kingdom. (2 Nephi 2:27-29)

Most Christians do not actually desire to obey God. They are *interested* in obeying God, but they allow their desire for other things to dictate their sinful behavior. Desire isn't the same as interest!

Most people get caught up in Jesus' godliness: the gospels are full of supernatural qualities. These qualities are wonderful, but they should not take away from his humanity. We can learn as much from Jesus' humanity as we can his godliness. Jesus is our Lord, Savior, and the son of God. While on the earth, he had incredible godly power to work miracles, and even had power given him over his own life. However, he did not have a superhuman power against sin. He was subject to all temptations of the flesh—in fact greater temptations than any other man. Yet, he was sinless. His sinlessness was not a manifestation of God, but a manifestation of righteous desire. No man will atone for the sins of the world. No man will resurrect himself. But all men can—and must—exercise the same desire to do God's will as Jesus possessed if they will be saved.

In this world, we can either choose good or evil. Those who choose good will be saved. Those who choose evil will not.

11 Now, concerning the state of the soul between death and the resurrection—Behold, it has been made known unto me by an angel, that the spirits of all men, as soon as they are departed from this mortal body, yea, the spirits of all men, whether they be good or evil, are taken home to that God who gave them life.

12 And then shall it come to pass, that the spirits of those who are righteous are received into a state of

happiness, which is called paradise, a state of rest, a state of peace, where they shall rest from all their troubles and from all care, and sorrow.

13 And then shall it come to pass, that the spirits of the wicked, yea, who are evil—for behold, they have no part nor portion of the Spirit of the Lord; for behold, *they chose evil works rather than good*; therefore the spirit of the devil did enter into them, and take possession of their house—and these shall be cast out into outer darkness; there shall be weeping, and wailing, and gnashing of teeth, and this *because of their own iniquity*, being led captive by the will of the devil.

14 Now this is the state of the souls of the wicked, yea, in darkness, and a state of awful, fearful looking for the fiery indignation of the wrath of God upon them; thus they remain in this state, as well as the righteous in paradise, until the time of their resurrection. (Alma 40)

You must choose to follow God in each choice, every time. You must deny yourself of all ungodliness, and every wordly lust, and keep all his commandments.

Therefore, if a man bringeth forth good works he hearkeneth unto the voice of the good shepard, and he doth follow him; but whosoever bringeth forth evil works, the same becometh a child of the devil, for he hearkeneth unto his voice, and doth follow him. (Alma 5:41)

We are told plainly that if we love God, we will keep his commandments:

15 If ye love me, keep my commandments.
16 And I will pray the Father, and he shall give you another Comforter, that he may abide with you for ever;
21 He that hath my commandments, and keepeth them, he it is that loveth me: and he that loveth me shall be loved of my Father, and I will love him, and will manifest myself to him.

71

23 Jesus answered and said unto him, If a man love me, he will keep my words: and my Father will love him, and we will come unto him, and make our abode with him. (John 14:15-16, 21, 23)

You cannot allow yourself to choose contrary to God's will, even if it costs you your life.

And thus we see that, when these Lamanites were brought to believe and to know the truth, they were firm, and would suffer even unto death rather than commit sin.... (Alma 24:19)

And they overcame him by the blood of the Lamb, and by the word of their testimony; and they loved not their lives unto the death. (Revelation 12:11)

34 ...Whosoever will come after me, let him deny himself, and take up his cross, and follow me.
35 For whosoever will save his life shall lose it; but whosoever shall lose his life for my sake and the gospel's, the same shall save it. (Mark 8)

You don't keep the commandments because of slight discomfort. How can you inherit the same glory as one who kept the commandments even though it cost his or her life? While the sacrifices God asks are different for every person, the common element is that each recipient is willing to obey God in all things, in all circumstances, until the end of their lives.

The atonement isn't magic: you really do have to change. The atonement is a ladder, given to us by Christ, allowing us to climb out of the consequences of the fall. You really do have to be everything that Jesus is asking you to be. There is no other way. The idea of meeting God halfway is false doctrine.

Dying in your sins

If you do not keep his commandments, it does not matter how much you say you believe in Jesus or how often you may engage in good works, you will die in your sins and be overwhelmed with grief and torment in his presence.

> And wo unto them who shall do these things away and die, for they die in their sins, and they cannot be saved in the kingdom of God; and I speak it according to the words of Christ; and I lie not. (Moroni 10:26)

> But wo unto him that has the law given, yea, that has all the commandments of God, like unto us, and that transgresseth them, and that wasteth the days of his probation, for awful is his state! (2 Nephi 9:27)

The punishment that awaits those who disobey God is not vengeful or arbitrary. It is simply the unavoidable result of natural law.

> 7 These are they that are redeemed of the Lord; yea, these are they that are taken out, that are delivered from that endless night of darkness; and thus they stand or fall; for behold, they are their own judges, whether to do good or do evil.
> 8 Now, the decrees of God are unalterable; therefore, the way is prepared that whosoever will may walk therein and be saved.
> 9 And now behold, my son, do not risk one more offense against your God upon those points of doctrine, which ye have hitherto risked to commit sin.
> 10 Do not suppose, because it has been spoken concerning restoration, that ye shall be restored from sin to happiness. Behold, I say unto you, wickedness never was happiness.
> 11 And now, my son, all men that are in a state of nature, or I would say, in a carnal state, are in the gall of bitterness and in the bonds of iniquity; they are without God in the world, and they have gone contrary to the nature of God; therefore, they are in a state contrary to the nature of happiness.
> 12 And now behold, is the meaning of the word restoration to take a thing of a natural state and place it

in an unnatural state, or to place it in a state opposite to its nature?

13 O, my son, this is not the case; but the meaning of the word restoration is to bring back again evil for evil, or carnal for carnal, or devilish for devilish—good for that which is good; righteous for that which is righteous; just for that which is just; merciful for that which is merciful. (Alma 41)

Unfortunately, death does not save you from your sins. If you have not reconciled your life to the commandments God has provided to you in this life, you will not be ready to meet God when you die, and you will remain in your present state:

And he doth not dwell in unholy temples; neither can filthiness or anything which is unclean be received into the kingdom of God; therefore I say unto you the time shall come, yea, and it shall be at the last day, that he who is filthy shall remain in his filthiness. (Alma 7:21)

Dying in one's sins relegates an individual to a state of suffering. Having rejected Jesus' sacrifice by disobeying his commandments to them, these individuals must suffer the penalty of their own sins:

33 Wherefore, if they should die in their wickedness they must be cast off also, as to the things which are spiritual, which are pertaining to righteousness; wherefore, they must be brought to stand before God, to be judged of their works; and if their works have been filthiness they must needs be filthy; and if they be filthy it must needs be that they cannot dwell in the kingdom of God; if so, the kingdom of God must be filthy also.

34 But behold, I say unto you, the kingdom of God is not filthy, and there cannot any unclean thing enter into the kingdom of God; wherefore there must needs be a place of filthiness prepared for that which is filthy.

35 And there is a place prepared, yea, even that awful hell of which I have spoken, and the devil is the preparator of it; wherefore the final state of the souls of

men is to dwell in the kingdom of God, or to be cast out because of that justice of which I have spoken.

36 Wherefore, the wicked are rejected from the righteous, and also from that tree of life, whose fruit is most precious and most desirable above all other fruits; yea, and it is the greatest of all the gifts of God. And thus I spake unto my brethren. Amen. (1 Nephi 15)

It is for this reason that God cast Adam and Eve out of the garden once they began to sin:

22 And the Lord God said, Behold, the man is become as one of us, to know good and evil: and now, lest he put forth his hand, and take also of the tree of life, and eat, and live for ever:

23 Therefore the Lord God sent him forth from the garden of Eden, to till the ground from whence he was taken.

24 So he drove out the man; and he placed at the east of the garden of Eden Cherubims, and a flaming sword which turned every way, to keep the way of the tree of life. (Genesis 3:22-24)

If Adam and Eve had eaten of the tree of life, they would have been permanently barred from God's presence because they would not have had the opportunity to repent. Through the resurrection, all men will be as immortal as Adam and Eve would have been if they had continued to eat of the tree of life. Therefore, this life is a time to repent and become sinless, because if we carry sin into the resurrection, we bar ourselves from God's presence eternally.

Because this is the state of those who did not repent in this life, it is incredibly important for us to reconcile ourselves to God's commandments in this life:

33 And now, as I said unto you before, as ye have had so many witnesses, therefore, I beseech of you that ye do not procrastinate the day of your repentance until the end; for after this day of life, which is given us to prepare for eternity, behold, if we do not improve our time while

in this life, then cometh the night of darkness wherein there can be no labor performed.

34 Ye cannot say, when ye are brought to that awful crisis, that I will repent, that I will return to my God. Nay, ye cannot say this; for that same spirit which doth possess your bodies at the time that ye go out of this life, that same spirit will have power to possess your body in that eternal world.

35 For behold, if ye have procrastinated the day of your repentance even until death, behold, ye have become subjected to the spirit of the devil, and he doth seal you his; therefore, the Spirit of the Lord hath withdrawn from you, and hath no place in you, and the devil hath all power over you; and this is the final state of the wicked.

36 And this I know, because the Lord hath said he dwelleth not in unholy temples, but in the hearts of the righteous doth he dwell; yea, and he has also said that the righteous shall sit down in his kingdom, to go no more out; but their garments should be made white through the blood of the Lamb. (Alma 34)

Keeping all of God's commandments is the only way to dwell in his presence.

21 Dear friends, if we feel at ease in the presence of God, we will have the courage to come near him.
22 He will give us whatever we ask, because we obey him and do what pleases him. (1 John 3, CEV)

20 For if our heart condemn us, God is greater than our heart, and knoweth all things.
21 Beloved, if our heart condemn us not, then have we confidence toward God.
22 And whatsoever we ask, we receive of him, because we keep his commandments, and do those things that are pleasing in his sight.
23 And this is his commandment, That we should believe on the name of his Son Jesus Christ, and love one another, as he gave us commandment.

24 And he that keepeth his commandments dwelleth in him, and he in him. And hereby we know that he abideth in us, by the Spirit which he hath given us. (1 John 3)

We must keep all of God's commandments, or we will find ourselves cast out of his presence after this life.

Wherefore, if ye have sought to do wickedly in the days of your probation, then ye are found unclean before the judgment-seat of God; and no unclean thing can dwell with God; wherefore, ye must be cast off forever. (1 Nephi 10:21)

Conversely, by keeping his commandments, we will find ourselves brought back into his presence.

Willful Disobedience

But behold, ye have rejected the truth, and rebelled against your holy God; and even at this time, instead of laying up for yourselves treasures in heaven, where nothing doth corrupt, and where nothing can come which is unclean, ye are heaping up for yourselves wrath against the day of judgment. (Helaman 8:25)

Sin is when we act contrary to our understanding of God's will. If we knowingly sin, we are in open rebellion against God; we are cut off from God and will be forever until we repent.

> But behold, and fear, and tremble before God, for ye ought to tremble; for the Lord redeemeth none such that rebel against him and die in their sins; yea, even all those that have perished in their sins ever since the world began, that have wilfully rebelled against God, that have known the commandments of God, and would not keep them; these are they that have no part in the first resurrection. (Mosiah 15:26)

Some seek to excuse themselves in willful disobedience by claiming that the blood of Jesus will save them in spite of their sin. Jesus cannot save his people *in* their sins. He can only save them *from* their sins.

> And, in fine, wo unto all those who die in their sins; for they shall return to God, and behold his face, and remain in their sins. (2 Nephi 9:38)

His sacrifice absolves the repentant from the penalty of their past sins. To absolve a man for his willful disobedience while he still persists in sin would be to deny the justice of God.

Personal repentance is required for one to be cleaned by the blood of Jesus:

> And I say unto you again that he cannot save them in their sins; for I cannot deny his word, and he hath said that no unclean thing can inherit the kingdom of heaven; therefore, how can ye be saved, except ye inherit the kingdom of heaven? Therefore, ye cannot be saved in your sins. (Alma 11:3)

Clearly, Jesus requires us to fully submit to him and his instructions to us. A partial sacrifice is not an acceptable one. The Lord does not forgive *a* sin. You won't find a single instance of his forgiving *a* sin in the entire canon. When he forgives you of your sins, he forgives you of all of them all at once. You can't repent of just one sin. You have to repent of *all* of your sins. "Therefore they did forsake *all* their sins, and their abominations, and their whoredoms, and did serve God with all diligence day and night." (3 Nephi 5:3)

Repentance is not just about forgiveness of sins. It is incomplete unless and until you have changed your attitude. True repentance occurs only when you completely subject yourself to God's will in your life. There are no partial sacrifices.

Too many people today believe that they can persist in disobeying God and still be saved. Their inheritance is hell:

> But behold, and fear, and tremble before God, for ye ought to tremble; for the Lord redeemeth none such that rebel against him and die in their sins; yea, even all those that have perished in their sins ever since the world began, *that have wilfully rebelled against God, that have known the commandments of God, and would not keep them*; these are they that have no part in the first resurrection. (Mosiah 15:26)

These must believe that somehow they will be able to lie to God on the judgment day, and stand up to his all-piercing eye, knowing full well that they rejected him and their chance at salvation:

15 Do you look forward with an eye of faith, and view this mortal body raised in immortality, and this corruption raised in incorruption, to stand before God to be judged according to the deeds which have been done in the mortal body?

16 I say unto you, can you imagine to yourselves that ye hear the voice of the Lord, saying unto you, in that day: Come unto me ye blessed, for behold, your works have been the works of righteousness upon the face of the earth?

17 Or do ye imagine to yourselves that ye can lie unto the Lord in that day, and say—Lord, our works have been righteous works upon the face of the earth—and that he will save you?

18 Or otherwise, can ye imagine yourselves brought before the tribunal of God with your souls filled with guilt and remorse, having a remembrance of all your guilt, yea, a perfect remembrance of all your wickedness, yea, a remembrance that ye have set at defiance the commandments of God?

19 I say unto you, can ye look up to God at that day with a pure heart and clean hands? I say unto you, can you look up, having the image of God engraven upon your countenances?

20 I say unto you, can ye think of being saved when you have yielded yourselves to become subjects to the devil?

21 I say unto you, ye will know at that day that ye cannot be saved; for there can no man be saved except his garments are washed white; yea, his garments must be purified until they are cleansed from all stain, through the blood of him of whom it has been spoken by our fathers, who should come to redeem his people from their sins.

22 And now I ask of you, my brethren, how will any of you feel, if ye shall stand before the bar of God, having your garments stained with blood and all manner of filthiness? Behold, what will these things testify against you?

23 Behold will they not testify that ye are murderers, yea, and also that ye are guilty of all manner of wickedness?
24 Behold, my brethren, do ye suppose that such an one can have a place to sit down in the kingdom of God, with Abraham, with Isaac, and with Jacob, and also all the holy prophets, whose garments are cleansed and are spotless, pure and white?
25 I say unto you, Nay; except ye make our Creator a liar from the beginning, or suppose that he is a liar from the beginning, ye cannot suppose that such can have place in the kingdom of heaven; but they shall be cast out for they are the children of the kingdom of the devil. (Alma 5)

Heaven's gates are closed tightly against all who willingly sin against God.

But wo, wo unto him who knoweth that he rebelleth against God! For salvation cometh to none such except it be through repentance and faith on the Lord Jesus Christ. (Mosiah 3:12)

But remember that he that persists in his own carnal nature, and goes on in the ways of sin and rebellion against God, remaineth in his fallen state and the devil hath all power over him. Therefore he is as though there was no redemption made, being an enemy to God; and also is the devil an enemy to God. (Mosiah 16:5)

Their experience in the day of judgment will be far different from their expectations:

1 And now, it came to pass that after Abinadi had spoken these words he stretched forth his hand and said: The time shall come when all shall see the salvation of the Lord; when every nation, kindred, tongue, and people shall see eye to eye and shall confess before God that his judgments are just.
2 And then shall the wicked be cast out, and they shall have cause to howl, and weep, and wail, and gnash their

teeth; and this because they would not hearken unto the voice of the Lord; therefore the Lord redeemeth them not.

3 For they are carnal and devilish, and the devil has power over them; yea, even that old serpent that did beguile our first parents, which was the cause of their fall; which was the cause of all mankind becoming carnal, sensual, devilish, knowing evil from good, subjecting themselves to the devil.

4 Thus all mankind were lost; and behold, they would have been endlessly lost were it not that God redeemed his people from their lost and fallen state.

5 But remember that he that persists in his own carnal nature, and goes on in the ways of sin and rebellion against God, remaineth in his fallen state and the devil hath all power over him. Therefore he is as though there was no redemption made, being an enemy to God; and also is the devil an enemy to God. (Mosiah 16:1-5)

Those who willingly disobey God are not only not saved, they also cut themselves off from the influence of the Spirit of God:

36 And now, I say unto you, my brethren, that after ye have known and have been taught all these things, if ye should transgress and go contrary to that which has been spoken, that ye do withdraw yourselves from the Spirit of the Lord, that it may have no place in you to guide you in wisdom's paths that ye may be blessed, prospered, and preserved—

37 I say unto you, that the man that doeth this, the same cometh out in open rebellion against God; therefore he listeth to obey the evil spirit, and becometh an enemy to all righteousness; therefore, the Lord has no place in him, for he dwelleth not in unholy temples.

38 Therefore if that man repenteth not, and remaineth and dieth an enemy to God, the demands of divine justice do awaken his immortal soul to a lively sense of his own guilt, which doth cause him to shrink from the presence of the Lord, and doth fill his breast with guilt,

and pain, and anguish, which is like an unquenchable fire, whose flame ascendeth up forever and ever.

39 And now I say unto you, that mercy hath no claim on that man; therefore his final doom is to endure a never-ending torment.

40 O, all ye old men, and also ye young men, and you little children who can understand my words, for I have spoken plainly unto you that ye might understand, I pray that ye should awake to a remembrance of the awful situation of those that have fallen into transgression. (Mosiah 2)

It is impossible for one in willful disobedience to come to know God. It is impossible for them to do the mighty works that are the privilege of all believers in Christ.

Part 2:

Walking with God

To Know Thee

And Enoch walked with God after he begat Methuselah
three hundred years, and begat sons and daughters:
(Genesis 5:22)

The Lord Jesus said that eternal life is to know the Father and the Son.

> And this is life eternal, that they might know thee the only true God, and Jesus Christ, whom thou hast sent. (John 17:3)

If you do not know God, you have not yet received eternal life. If you do, you have. The logic here is simple and clear. But what does it mean to know God? If eternal life means to know God, then what could be more important than first understanding what it means to know God and then coming to that point?

John taught that those who know God keep his commandments:

> 3 And hereby we do know that we know him, if we keep his commandments.
> 4 He that saith, I know him, and keepeth not his commandments, is a liar, and the truth is not in him. (1 John 2)

He equated keeping his commandments to being sinless:

> Whosoever abideth in him sinneth not: whosoever sinneth hath not seen him, neither known him. (1 John 3:6)

Part 1 describes the process of becoming sinless. While this is a prerequisite for knowing God, it is not a good descriptor for what it actually means to know him. Reconciling yourself to God through repentance makes it possible for us to begin the process of coming to know God.

To know God, you must have met him. You cannot say you know someone if you have never met them.

To know God, you must have met him many times. You can't say you know someone who you have only met once. Knowing someone means you know what they look like and what their voice sounds like. It means you've spent a great deal of time with them, and you know what pleases them and puts them off.

To know God, you must not only have seen him multiple times, but you must spend quite a bit of time with him. No matter how far this may seem from your reality, it is essential to describe in order for you to grasp the magnitude of the journey you are about to begin.

Is it possible to know God in this life? There are many people who believe it is not possible to see God. There are many others who think it is a very rare experience, or perhaps an experience reserved only for a select few. They are all wrong.

You *can* see God, you *can* talk with him face to face, and you *can* spend enough time with him that your relationship with him becomes the cornerstone of your life. You can do this no matter who you are, what your past is, or how spiritual you are, because this supernal privilege is ours not because of who we are, but because of who he is. He is that good. He is that powerful. He is mighty to save all his children if they will but believe in him.

It should not be surprising that almost all deny the possibility of such a relationship with God. Since the Lord said there would only be a few who would figure out the path to him (see Matthew 7:14), the dissent of the majority should stoke our consideration rather than squelch it. If you peel away the hearts of those who claim that such experiences are not possible, you will find that the key reason most say it is not possible to know God in the normal sense of the word is that *their* efforts to do so have not proved successful. As with the idea of becoming sinless, where similar arguments exist, the only thing their failure proves is that *their* tactics do not work, not that the outcome is impossible. One thing you can be sure of: if you follow the doctrines of those who claim it is not possible, you will surely prove them right!

It *is* possible to be sinless in this life, and it *is* possible to know God in this life. Beyond being possible, achieving these two states is actually the purpose of this life.

While the scriptures give volumes of evidence that God was right when he said that few find the path to eternal life, they also provide examples of several people who were successful in their quest. We need not imagine what it means to know God. We find the condition explained through the lives of Adam, Seth, Enoch, Noah, Melchizedek, Abraham, Isaac, Jacob, Joseph, Moses, Joshua, Elijah, Elisha, Isaiah, Jeremiah, Peter, Paul, and many others. What did their collective experience entail? They saw God face to face and were conversant with him. God spoke with them, and they spoke with God. Their prayers were answered. They had great internal peace. They had a passionate love for God, and a consummate trust in God. They were taught great mysteries. They communed with angels. They worked mighty miracles. They were given specific missions from God. They knew God well and were known by God.

We are too quick to dismiss these men as the exception rather than the rule. The only thing exceptional about them was their desire toward the Lord. Desire toward God is not a fixed property. It is a characteristic that is developed commensurate with the heed and diligence we choose to exert. Since God is good, those who seek him will learn of his goodness, causing them to want to seek him even more. We choose, through how much heed and diligence we exert, how much desire we have towards God. The only thing keeping you from the lives these men lived is your choices.

These men were not blessed with special circumstances. Enoch had a young family when he began walking with the Lord. Peter was a successful businessman when he began walking with God. David was a lowly shepherd. Abraham was the son of an idol maker. You and I possess every opportunity to mimic their actions, and because God is no respecter of persons, if we do, we will receive the same results.

The lives of these men were full of the outcomes of successful gospel living. But what was the process? Christianity is meant to be the process of achieving these outcomes—of coming to know and commune with God—yet almost everyone fails to achieve these outcomes. We can hardly blame unbelievers for failing to embrace Christianity. As Paul said of the Jews, our failure to obtain the fruits of the gospel turns away those who might otherwise believe (see Romans 2:21-24).

Christianity is meant to bring an individual up to the point where they walk with God. Modern Christianity has almost entirely failed to do that. It has lost the root process that makes it possible. It was not always this way. The scriptures are full of people who managed to attain experiences with God beyond our collective imagination. What happened? *Christianity has systematically eroded from a relationship to a religion.* Core, efficacious principles have been replaced with traditions that fail to produce the fruits described in the scriptures. A relationship with God has been replaced with to do lists of rules and works.

Walking with God comes as a result of learning efficacious versions of what most Christians think they already know: repentance (covered in Part 1), prayer, and worship (covered here). Please do not assume that your familiarity with these words indicates your familiarity with their meaning. As you will see by reading this book, the devil has gained a great victory by hijacking and neutering the original meanings of prayer and worship. By practicing these elements in the form of the ancients, anyone can achieve the same kind of relationship they had with God—not through some sort of conjuring, but as the natural consequence of divinely appointed law.

Walking with God will occur for you as you move closer and closer to him. I have seen many paintings of the following description in Revelation:

> Behold, I stand at the door, and knock: if any man hear my voice, and open the door, I will come in to him, and will sup with him, and he with me. (Revelation 3:20)

The door analogy does not tell the whole story. Really, it is more like a ladder. The Lord stands at the top, and calls down to us: "Come up! Come up!" Meanwhile, most Christians are content to completely ignore the ladder. Others venture over to it and earnestly call: "Come down!" "Come down"! The only way we can come closer to God is by climbing up the ladder. We climb the ladder by reaching out to God through first reconciling ourselves to him in repentance, and then through communing with him in prayer and worship.

The difference between normal life and walking with God is represented in the story of the Lord's return to hostile Bethany after the death of Lazarus. Mary, Martha, and Lazarus were not reprobate atheists. They were devout disciples of the Lord. However, they did not accompany him in his ministry. When Lazarus grew sick, Mary and Martha sent a message to the Lord:

> 3 Therefore his sisters sent unto him, saying, Lord, behold, he whom thou lovest is sick.
> 4 When Jesus heard that, he said, This sickness is not unto death, but for the glory of God, that the Son of God might be glorified thereby. (John 11)

The record says that "Jesus loved Martha, and her sister, and Lazarus." (John 11:5) His disciples were amazed that he was willing to return to Bethany to heal Lazarus, as the Jews sought openly to kill him. The Lord explained his love for Mary, Martha, and Lazarus motivated him to share with them some of the blessings that the disciples who accompanied him had received, despite what it would require:

> 9 Jesus answered, Are there not twelve hours in the day? If any man walk in the day, he stumbleth not, because he seeth the light of this world.
> 10 But if a man walk in the night, he stumbleth, because there is no light in him.
> 11 These things said he: and after that he saith unto them, Our friend Lazarus sleepeth; but I go, that I may awake him out of sleep.
> 12 Then said his disciples, Lord, if he sleep, he shall do well.
> 13 Howbeit Jesus spake of his death: but they thought that he had spoken of taking of rest in sleep.
> 14 Then said Jesus unto them plainly, Lazarus is dead.
> 15 And I am glad for your sakes that I was not there, to the intent ye may believe; nevertheless let us go unto him.
> 16 Then said Thomas, which is called Didymus, unto his fellowdisciples, Let us also go, that we may die with him. (John 11)

Like Martha, Mary, and Lazarus, Christians who believe in God but do not yet walk with him do not yet "walk in the day." All of us can. If the Lord was willing to return to Bethany despite the hazards to his life, he is willing to come to any of us, if we but love him as Lazarus, Mary, and

Martha loved him. We choose to walk in the day when we allow God to show us all of our sins and repent of them, no matter what it requires.

> 17 For God sent not his Son into the world to condemn the world; but that the world through him might be saved.
> 18 He that believeth on him is not condemned: but he that believeth not is condemned already, because he hath not believed in the name of the only begotten Son of God.
> 19 And this is the condemnation, that *light is come into the world, and men loved darkness rather than light,* because their deeds were evil.
> 20 For *every one that doeth evil hateth the light, neither cometh to the light, lest his deeds should be reproved.*
> 21 But he that doeth truth cometh to the light, that his deeds may be made manifest, that they are wrought in God. (John 3)

As you draw closer to God, you will enjoy increased interaction with him. Your experiences with him will grow from feeling impressions to receiving strong, clear information through the Holy Ghost. You will come to hear the Lord's audible voice. You will interact with angels. You will see the Lord. You will speak with him face to face. These things will happen more frequently. Eventually, he will introduce you to the Father. Eventually, you will enjoy constant access to God. Your relationship with him will be more real than anything else in your life, and you will comprehend the true meaning of building your life upon the rock of the Lord Jesus Christ. He will be an anchor to your soul, a rock solid foundation in your life, and a brilliant source of light that illuminates every aspect of every day of your life.

Though the exact unfolding of these experiences seems custom fit for each individual, the general experience is the same. You progress from one level of experience with God to another. Your relationship with him will develop from being his servant, to his son or daughter, to his friend.

Walking with God refers both to this transitional process and its eventual outcome. Walking with God is very different from the normal Christian life. The normal Christian's interaction with God is limited to a few occasional and brief encounters with his spirit. Even those few who have seen Jesus once cannot say they really know him. To know God, you must acquire a habitation with him. What does this mean?

Consider the Lord's teachings in John 14. Here, he describes three degrees of relationship with God:

> 16 And I will pray the Father, and he shall give you another Comforter, that he may abide with you for ever;
> 17 Even the Spirit of truth; whom the world cannot receive, because it seeth him not, neither knoweth him: but ye know him; for he dwelleth with you, and shall be in you.
> 21 He that hath my commandments, and keepeth them, he it is that loveth me: and he that loveth me shall be loved of my Father, and I will love him, and will manifest myself to him.
> 23 Jesus answered and said unto him, If a man love me, he will keep my words: and my Father will love him, and we will come unto him, and make our abode with him. (John 14)

The first degree of relationship with God is to have the Holy Ghost dwell with you (16-17). The second is to have the Lord manifest himself to you (21). This is a *visitation*. This is the relationship that Mary, Martha, and Lazarus had. The third is to have the Lord abide with you (23). This third degree of relationship is a *habitation*.

While communion through the Holy Ghost is wonderful, it is not the same as a face-to-face seeing and hearing experience. While a visitation is a once off or occasional event, a habitation is constant. Most Christians recognize that the Holy Ghost can be our constant companion. Few Christians realize that we can also have the Lord himself to be our constant companion. This is what it means to have a habitation with God.

God's greatest desire is for everyone to have eternal life. You cannot reach that fullness without also receiving a habitation with God. God's greatest desire, therefore, is for everyone to know him just as well as scriptural personalities did and do. Though it would sooth our conscience to imagine a way for us to know God as well as those in the scriptures without any of their experiences, that is simply not the case. Just as a stick has two ends, you cannot know God as well as those in the scriptures without having the same degree and frequency of experiences they had with God.

Imagine what it would be like to see the Lord Jesus and speak with him every time you pray. This is the relationship that Moses had with God. But he was not the only one. David had a habitation with God. He said "...I foresaw the Lord always before my face, for he is on my right hand, that I should not be moved:" (Acts 2:25) What if they were not the only ones? What if the key to understanding why the experiences in the scriptures are so rare in normal life is to realize that the underlying relationship these people had with God was fundamentally different than the relationship you have with God?

It is possible to know God in this life. It is possible to always have interactive prayers, where you have conversations and not one-way monologues. It is possible to frequently see and talk with God face-to-face. It is possible to have God frequently reveal to you new mysteries through inspiration, voices, dreams, visions, and visitations. It is possible to be commanded to call down mighty miracles from heaven. It is possible to be a frequent visitor in heaven.

Knowing God means having daily interactions with him. It means being not only *as* familiar with the spiritual realm as the natural realm, but *more* familiar with the spiritual realm than the natural realm. If that sounds grandiose, it should. "...Eye hath not seen, nor ear heard, neither have entered into the heart of man, the things which God hath prepared for them that love him." (1 Corinthians 2:9) Elisha had more perception of the spiritual realm than the natural. When surrounded by an army sent to kill him, he saw legions of angels sent to protect him, and did not worry. When Elijah needed guidance, he saw God's hand causing natural wonders, then heard God's audible voice bringing him the peace he needed despite those who sought his life. When Stephen was stoned for preaching the gospel, he saw an open vision of the throne of God.

Do you live in the spiritual realm? Do you have daily experiences with God? Do you go into his presence often? Do you have communion with angels? Are your spiritual eyes open to see God's work in your life and in the world? Rather than only reading about these things, God is calling you to experience them. He is calling you to claim the inheritance of the saints: a true connection with heaven more real than anything in this fleeting, fallen world. This is the extraordinary blessing available to all Christians: to know God, to commune with angels, to be taken up into heaven, to frequently associate with angels, and to be an integral part of God's functioning kingdom on earth and in heaven.

It is God's will to abide with all of his children. This is not meant to be an experience for the select few. The Lord's only condition is that we love him and keep his words. All those who love the Lord and keep his words can have a habitation with God.

Knowing God is not only possible in this life, it is the purpose of this life. We came to this earth to come up to that level of interaction with God.

These experiences are not optional fringe benefits of living the gospel of Jesus Christ. They are not rare occurrences reserved for the few or elite. They are *always* present in the lives of those who are inheritors of eternal life. The absence of this degree of interaction with God indicates that an individual has deviated from the life required of those who will inherit eternal life.

This is the inheritance of the servants of God, and yet so very few of us have risen to the mark. For some, it is because they do not believe these blessings are possible. For others, they do not experience these blessings simply because they do not know where to find them. The rest of the chapters in this book address both obstacles by explaining these blessings and describing how they are encountered.

Connecting to Heaven

And he dreamed, and behold a ladder set up on the earth, and the top of it reached to heaven: and behold the angels of God ascending and descending on it. (Genesis 28:12)

We live in a fallen world. This dark world does not supply the power and glory necessary to live a godly life. Everything that is good in this world is a product of a higher world. Miracles do not pertain to this world. Happiness does not pertain to this world. Citizens of this earth are subjects to its king, the devil. If left to only what this world provides, all men would be miserable, broken, suffering creatures.

Heaven, in contrast to this world, is a place of miracles, goodness, happiness, and light. Citizens of heaven are subjects to its king, God. Those who do God's work on this earth must draw from the power of heaven. By doing so, they can serve as a conduit through which God manifests his goodness and power here on earth.

There are many Biblical accounts of the Lord leaving his disciples and spending the very early morning or late evening in prayer. Jesus would go off to solitary places to pray early in the morning (see Mark 1:35 and Luke 4:42). He would make sure he was alone, and arrange for that in spite of multitudes of people and his disciples following him everywhere he went (see Mark 6:45-46, Luke 5:16, and Matthew 14:23). He sometimes spent the whole night in prayer (see Luke 6:12). He put aside his daily work to make sure he had time to focus on uninterrupted prayer (see Mark 1:36-37). He spent a considerable time in prayer.

Why did the Lord Jesus pray so often and for so long? The Lord's mission was to bring light into this dark world. He had to pull the light from heaven (see Luke 22:41-43). As a mortal, he was a conduit for transmitting that light from heaven to earth (see Luke 8:46).

The Lord was like a battery for light. His righteousness gave him capacity, and his interaction with heaven filled that capacity. His daily work depleted his stores of light. As he went about daily doing the works of his Father, virtue went out of him (see Luke 8:46). As he was bombarded by unbelief, false accusations, and persecution, his light was attenuated. The Lord's light was finite while housed in a mortal body. It constantly decayed in the darkness of this fallen world. He had to charge his spiritual batteries frequently. As he routinely connected to heaven in prayer, he was recharged and able to continue providing a heavenly example that transcended anything any man had done previously (see John 15:24). If he had not connected with heaven as often and intensely as he had, he would not have been able to do the miracles that he did.

Like the Savior, we can charge our capacity to radiate God's goodness through frequent, intense interaction with him. The Lord Jesus came to earth as the Son of Man in order to show us that it was possible as a son of man to do all the things he did. He instructed his followers to do all the things he did (see John 14:12). When men become vessels of the glory of God and transmit God's goodness to others, it depletes them. To do God's works here on earth, we must establish and maintain a connection to heaven.

Moses showed this pattern. He spent much time in the Holy of Holies in the temple, and on several occasions went into a high mountain to connect to heaven. Returning from these occasions, he brought back a little of heaven with him in the form of communications from heaven, power from heaven, and even the physical manifestation of God's glory upon him. Because of his private sacrifice, he was able to publicly bless the children of Israel with far more of God's glory than they would have enjoyed in his absence.

The Lord and Moses were special people with special missions, but do we have any reason to believe that God will use anyone miraculously no matter their particular circumstances? The mission of the Lord and Moses were singular, but the means they used to accomplish these missions were not special. We have the same means available, and if we are willing to use them, God will use us in great power to do his work just as he did with others.

Your mission in life relies just as much on obtaining a connection with God as Moses' mission did. The way Moses approached God is open for anyone who will obey God's commandments, and anyone who approaches God in the same way as Moses will work just as great miracles as Moses did. Moses' greatness was not the cause of his great works—God's greatness was. Anyone who connects to the God of Moses will work mighty miracles—whether they be public or private.

Why isn't this connection a common experience? There is a barrier between us and heaven created by the fall of Adam. This barrier is two-fold, created both by our individual sin, and existing generally due to the fallen state of this world. In the garden of Eden, neither of these conditions were existent, and God visited this world freely. Adam had constant access to him. In our fallen world, by default our access to God is limited. However, because of the Lord Jesus Christ, who conquered sin and death, the barrier between the two worlds can be broken.

If the barrier is penetrable, why have so few broken through to enjoy constant interaction with God? Because the way to break through is not generally known. Though described plainly in the scriptures, the false traditions of faithless men have warped our ability to read God's word literally to the point where we need help to peel the scales of unbelief from our eyes and see the path God has described to us from the beginning. Truly, he stands at the door and knocks. In other words, the Lord Jesus has already worked out the path for us to connect with heaven and come up to a constant, full interaction with him. Our body, mind, and soul reside here, in a lower estate than God and many of his angels. It is as if he has created a ladder and lowered it into our pit, and is calling us to climb it.

This analogy is quite fitting, as it reminds us of Jacob's ladder. Jacob once saw the ascent and descent of heavenly beings to and from earth:

> And he dreamed, and behold a ladder set up on the earth, and the top of it reached to heaven: and behold the angels of God ascending and descending on it. (Genesis 28:12)

Jacob's ladder and the Lord's door (see Revelation 3:20) are actually not ladders or doors, but different names for the same portal. This is the portal that connects you to heaven. Whether seen or unseen, a connection to heaven is like an electrical circuit. It is an open pathway for light to flow from heaven to you.

Most Christians have, at some point in their lives, received a sudden burst of light from God. Like an electrical arc from a ground to a battery, you can receive bursts of contact with God whenever you momentarily get close enough to God. A habitation with God, on the other hand, is like a permanent connection to the battery that you can switch on at any time. You can come up to the point where this conduit is no longer temporary. You can come to the point where you can instantly be in heaven or see the Lord before you at any time and in any place—a habitation with God. In a sense, you can become a conduit from heaven to earth. This is what it means for God to abide in you, and you in him. This happens when your spirit increases in glory, becoming capable of constant interaction with the glory of God.

When you keep all of God's commandments, the portal opens, and you gain access to the heavens. That succinct description of the way may tempt you to think it is easy. The way is certainly simple. Yet, there is nothing more difficult in this world. There are several significant barriers to encountering God.

Our traditions keep us from encountering God. The traditions of men pull us away from the path that leads to encountering God. This should come as no surprise, given that encountering God is always a minority experience, and traditions are formed by the majority. In the smokescreen of tradition, the only way to find the truth is to feel one's way through patiently and steadfastly seeking, obtaining, and trying the putative word of God. This process is described later in this book.

The world keeps us from encountering God. Though the process of coming to God is simple, it requires consummate desire and attention. Seeking God cannot be a part-time profession. The world demands our daily, constant focus. Those who successfully encounter God must consciously choose to subject every day to him, even while shouldering the temporal burdens of mortal life. Instead of seeing the gospel as a subset of life, life is seen as a subset of the gospel. This doesn't mean that one must live in a cave to meet God. Surrender doesn't always mean walking away. Many times it means to walk with a different purpose. Seeking God consists primarily of one's inward purpose. Though outer behavior will change, it is not always perceptible to the outside world, even when it makes a mighty change in the spiritual realm that surrounds us.

Throughout this book, the keys of establishing and growing a conduit from you to God are discussed. You will learn how to worship God and how to wait upon God. You will learn how to pray and what to pray for. You will learn how to develop compassion by interceding for others. If you apply these keys, you will come to the point where you have a habitation with God. You will pray and receive answers to your prayers. Your spiritual eyes will open. You will come to see the effects of the spiritual realm on your everyday life, and learn to effect change by working through prayer. You will have constant access to the Lord Jesus and you will be taken to meet the Father.

Interacting with Heaven

---

*For the invisible things of him from the creation of the
world are clearly seen... (Romans 1:20)*

There are two parts to our mortal existence. The first part is what
we experience with the physical senses. It consists of what we see, hear,
and touch in our physical body. This is the world we know from birth.
The second part of our mortal existence is unseen, yet it can be seen. It
is unheard, yet it can be heard. It is untouched, yet it can be felt. This is
the spirit realm.

Though men by default do not perceive or acknowledge it, the
spirit realm is real. Before this world existed physically, it existed
spiritually. It was from that realm that God spoke and brought the
physical world into existence. Because the physical was created by the
spiritual, the spiritual realm is greater than the physical world we live in.

Everything we experience pertaining to this world is experienced
in our physical bodies. Yet, our physical bodies are not our entire selves.
Erroneously thinking they are leads many people to lives absent the
glories of heaven and full of suffering. This world is no different.

Just as each of us has a physical body and a spirit, this world is
comprised of spiritual and physical portions. The world works the same
way we do: what happens in the physical realm cannot be separated from
what happens in the spiritual realm. They are intertwined, and
understanding how each effects the other is crucial to living the way God
intended.

Imagine driving a car with black paint covering all the windows.
You would be able to start, propel, and steer the car, but you'd have no
idea where you were going or whether you have arrived. You would have
to drive very slowly, and you would have no idea what was happening
or why when you unavoidably collided with other objects. Trying to live

in and understand the world with physical perception only is like trying to drive a car with opaque windows.

What happens in the physical world is mostly just the visible effect of what is happening in the spiritual realm. Awareness of the spiritual realm will grant you an understanding of just how much of what happens in the physical world is a product of what happens in the spiritual realm. A perception of the spiritual realm will enable you to act in the full breadth that God intended and empower you to have a much bigger impact on your life and the lives of others.

The vast majority of men bumble through life blissfully unaware of the greater half of mortal existence. Like children, they exist in a world they do not understand. Much of our frustrations and our failure to achieve our godly potential lies in our ignorance of the existence of the spirit realm and how to interact with it. As children of God, every person on this earth was created to act, not to be acted upon. And yet, if you do not understand or perceive the spiritual realm, you are quite limited in how you can act and react to the events around you.

We operate ineffectively in the spirit realm because we try to interact with it from earth. That relationship is backwards because everything on earth, being a lower degree of glory, is governed by what happens in the spirit realm, consisting of the higher degrees of glory. When we effect the natural realm through working in the spirit realm, we can infuse God's goodness and glory into earth life, which is naturally of a lower, fallen estate, and walk in mighty works of God and in constant companionship with him and his light. To operate only in the natural realm is to be a serf in God's kingdom—living out the doldrums of life without an awareness of greater things or how the world really works. The more we learn about how to operate in the spirit realm, the more we learn to have a real, powerful effect on bringing God's will to pass on earth as it is in heaven. We grow from a blind, dumb, deaf baby incapable of acting for itself into a fully functioning agent on the Lord's errand.

As Christians, we strive to be God's soldiers on earth. Yet, if we do not understand or perceive the spiritual realm, we are quite limited in what we can do. Like a sailor in a war fought mostly on land, if we want to fight, we need to expand our capabilities to operate in the spirit realm.

This world is not the real world. The spirit realm is the real world. This world is just a lower realm controlled to a great extent by what happens in the spirit realm. Living here without knowing about or being able to work in the spirit realm is like being an animal in a cage, fully subjected to the evil rulers of this world. If you do not know who controls you, and how they control you, how can you gain power over them?

God wants you to understand the spirit realm. Paul contrasted the physical life with the spiritual. Referring to the Israelites in the wilderness he said, "For ye are not come unto the mount that might be touched, and that burned with fire, nor unto blackness, and darkness, and tempest." (Hebrews 12:18) At that time, the Israelites lived a law of carnal commandments housed in the physical realm. Paul contrasted this with a charge to come up to something higher: "But ye are come unto mount Sion, and unto the city of the living God, the heavenly Jerusalem, and to an innumerable company of angels." (Hebrews 12:22)

We are meant to ascend to a spiritual existence. We are meant to ascend from canned commandments to a living, interactive existence with God. We are meant to see as we are seen. The only way for that to happen is for you to see the spirit realm. God wants you to be able to see the spirit realm. He wants you to see eye to eye (Isaiah 52:8), or see the same things, as those who have seen heaven, who see him, and who see angels.

The Lord can open your spiritual eyes. The Lord opens the eyes of the physically blind when they ask him to do so. Won't he do the same for those who are spiritually blind? The Lord once partially healed a blind man, who first received blurry vision. He can do this momentarily, granting a vision or visitation to you, to entice you to seek more. Don't stop there! Rattle the gates of heaven until he fully and permanently opens your spiritual eyes!

As your spiritual eyes open, you will start to become aware of what is happening in the spiritual realm. What you comprehend in the spiritual realm will inform your behaviors and attitudes in the physical realm. Seeing the spiritual realm is not about entertainment or curiosity. Rather, these experiences are to communicate knowledge and provide opportunities for supernatural action. Working in the spiritual realm makes it possible for you, as an individual and a nobody, to effect outcomes that are hard to overstate.

So much of what we war against in this world is actually spiritual in nature. Because we don't initially see the actuating forces, we lose sight of that fact.

How many of our worldly conflicts are actually spiritual in their root? Demons can cause physical outcomes: they tempt men to sin, inspire caustic human relationships, create physical sickness, and much more. Similarly, angels can inspire men toward God, mend hearts, enlighten minds, heal ailments, and much more. For too long, demons have had free reign to operate on us, our children, and our neighbors while we fruitlessly cut the heads off the hydra of symptoms in the physical realm, of what are truly spiritual diseases.

It is time for Christians to understand and use the power and authority the Lord has given them. We are using the wrong weapons in many of the battles we wage. Paul understood the supremacy of the spirit realm. He said:

> For we wrestle not against flesh and blood, but against principalities, against powers, against the rulers of the darkness of this world, against spiritual wickedness in high places. (Ephesians 6:12)

He was not saying that we do not have problems in the physical world of flesh and blood. He was saying that all problems in the physical world have roots in the spiritual realm.

Comprehending the spiritual realm causes us to react differently to our physical circumstances. When Paul feared for the state of the ship he was on, he was soothed not by the physical world, but the spiritual realm. An angel visited him and told him that all passengers would survive. When Daniel faced being eaten alive by lions, he did not engage the lions physically. Instead, he knelt down and prayed. Can you imagine yourself in this situation? Would your first instinct be to look for a makeshift weapon, to cower in fear, or to pray? Daniel was protected through spiritual intervention. He understood that his problem, like all problems, was not physical in its root, but spiritual. He reacted accordingly.

So often, we rage against our circumstances in the physical world without realizing that if we glimpsed the full picture the spiritual realm provides, we would gracefully accept what is actually completely for our good. If we are keeping all of God's commandments, we can trust that God is doing something good for us, even if we do not perceive the goodness. "And we know that all things work together for good to them that love God, to them who are the called according to his purpose." (Romans 8:28) By recognizing that there is good in everything that happens to us, even if we don't perceive it, we invite God to open our eyes to the truth. "And the light shineth in darkness; and the darkness comprehended it not." (John 1:5) Even when all we see is darkness, the light is still shining. We just don't comprehend it. It is impossible for the darkness to overcome the light (see John 1:5, AMP). It is impossible for anything in this world to overcome the good God has set up as the eventual outcome of what may seem like an endless chain of trials.

> Nor height, nor depth, nor any other creature, shall be able to separate us from the love of God, which is in Christ Jesus our Lord. (Romans 8:39)

With an awareness of the light comes a perception of the darkness. Those whose perception is limited to the physical realm recognize only the outwardly obvious places where Satan reigns: nightclubs, gambling halls, strip clubs, bars, and inner city street corners. As your spiritual eyes open, you will marvel at what places are strongholds of the enemy despite no indication in the natural. As just one example, consider college university campuses. While most realize that college students' lives are infiltrated by porn, sex, drugs, and evil ideologies, few comprehend that most university professors are as demon possessed as their pupils, and are as depraved in morals as much as they are in common sense, as their lives are devoid of light.

Our spirits can intensify to the point that wherever we go we effect our environment without even noticing it. Peter was so infused with the Lord's spirit that his presence resulted in healing the sick without even touching them:

> 15 Insomuch that they brought forth the sick into the streets, and laid them on beds and couches, that at the least the shadow of Peter passing by might overshadow some of them.
> 16 There came also a multitude out of the cities round about unto Jerusalem, bringing sick folks, and them which were vexed with unclean spirits: and they were healed every one. (Acts 5:15-16)

Paul was so infused with the Lord's spirit that his personal articles had power over demons.

> 11 And God wrought special miracles by the hands of Paul:

12 So that from his body were brought unto the sick handkerchiefs or aprons, and the diseases departed from them, and the evil spirits went out of them. (Acts 19)

As your spiritual eyes open, you will perceive as demons flee from the light that emanates from you as one of God's servants. Your home will become a refuge from the demon saturated world. When you arrive at your place of work, you will drive away and keep at bay the forces of Satan. When you travel, your presence will chase away the demons that have made a stronghold out of the places you visit.

The Lord will use you in sophisticated plans to provide opportunities for his children to be emancipated from darkness and to embrace light. Sometimes, you'll be shown the amazing and astonishing details of these plans. Other times, you will be aware that you are being used, but unaware of the consequences in the lives of others. At still other times, you will be oblivious to what is happening in spite of the magnitude of the effects of God's light in you.

Demons stand up and take notice of God's servants. The opposition you will encounter will come in equal proportion to the light you receive. This is addressed in a later chapter.

The spirit realm provides a more effective—if nontraditional—approach to problems. If you were given the task of conquering a city with hardened, impenetrable defenses, how would you do it? The allied forces in WWII broke through the German resistance at Normandy with staggering losses. They pitted flesh against bullets and bunkers, and paid a terrible price. Ancient Israel's military victories, on the other hand, demonstrate the power of working in the spirit realm. The Israelites conquered Jericho, a supposedly unconquerable city, without the recorded loss of a single life. They did it not with military might, but by working in the spirit realm. The Israelites conquered Jericho in 7 days. For the first 6 days, they did not engage in any war. Instead, they focused on God, carrying the ark of the covenant around the city once per day. On the seventh day, God miraculously knocked down the thick walls of the city, and they ravaged the previously impenetrable city in a day. How long would it have taken with conventional means? Would it even have been possible?

What are the Jerichos in your life? How have you been attacking them? It does not matter how temporal the matter at hand may seem, fighting it in the spiritual realm will reveal root causes you had not considered and will yield results that were otherwise impossible.

There is an apocryphal quote attributed to Abraham Lincoln where he states that if he had four hours to cut down a tree, he'd spend three of those hours sharpening his axe. Anyone who has tried it can tell you that chopping down a tree with a dull axe is a disaster. The axe handle might go before the tree does! When we are ignorant of the spiritual realm, we spend far more effort on the physical realm than is necessary, and achieve far fewer goals than we could if we had simply put sufficient effort into tackling the matter in the spirit realm first.

The key tool for interacting with the spirit realm is prayer. God can open our spiritual eyes in visions, our ears to hearing voices, and our minds through quickened flashes of knowledge, but we cannot initiate any of those experiences directly. Desire is often required, but it is never sufficient. Real experiences from God cannot be conjured by desire or imagination alone. They must come from God. God grants these experiences to the degree that you reconcile yourself to his will and character.

After you have repented of all your sins, the best way to work in the spirit realm is through prayer. Prayer is how we initiate communication with God and one means to subject ourselves to his will.

Prayer opens the eyes of our spiritual understanding. If we want to see the unseen, we ask in prayer. If we want to know what we do not know, we ask in prayer. If we need to summon the assistance of angels, we ask in prayer. Our frequent practice of prayer opens, expands, and persists our connection with God, making his communications with us more frequent, whether his responses come during our prayers or between them.

God administers the universe through the angels that stand by his throne and are distributed throughout his kingdom:

> And he said, Hear thou therefore the word of the Lord: I saw the Lord sitting on his throne, and all the host of heaven standing by him on his right hand and on his left. (1 Kings 22:19)

Every level of God's government has an angel in charge, and each governing angel has angels under his charge. This pattern continues both in heavenly realms and here on earth. For example, each region on earth has a chief angel. In fact, each person has an angel assigned to them. As you can imagine, that adds up to a lot of angels. They are innumerable:

> And I beheld, and I heard the voice of many angels round about the throne and the beasts and the elders: and the number of them was ten thousand times ten thousand, and thousands of thousands; (Revelation 5:11)

These angels don't simply sit idle. They conduct God's work.

With angels being the agents of God's work, and with so many of them, it should come as no surprise that they are intimately involved in the daily affairs of life on earth. The spiritual realm is the realm of angels. If you desire to do God's work, you must learn to work in the spiritual realm. If you desire to work in the spiritual realm, you must learn to work with the angels.

Interactions with angels are key to our work in the spirit realm. Angels are critical agents in God's plan, yet they operate outside of the awareness of most Christians. It ought not to be this way.

The interplay between your standing with God and an angel's standing with God determines how you will interact with them. We are told that men are a little lower than the angels (Psalm 8:5), but we are also told that men will judge angels (1 Corinthians 6:3). Which is it? Actually, both are true. Angels, men, and demons each come in all degrees of power. Some have attained great power, and stand in the presence of God. Gabriel, for instance, said that he stands in the presence of God (Luke 1:19). As an angel, the devil obtained power to stand in the presence of God (Job 1:6). Some angels are high ranking, some are lower ranking, and many angels fall somewhere in between. In some cases, angels will appear to you and you will give them God's instructions. In many cases, angels will appear to you to give you God's instructions. Sometimes, you will work alongside angels in carrying out God's instructions. In all cases, angels are agents of God's will. They are not objects of worship, and they are not replacements for God himself.

A case study in interacting with angels is provided by Paul's call to go to Macedonia. After preaching the gospel in several cities, he was searching for where to preach next. He suggested options and was rebutted by the Holy Ghost:

> 6 Now when they had gone throughout Phrygia and the region of Galatia, and were forbidden of the Holy Ghost to preach the word in Asia,

> 7 After they were come to Mysia, they assayed to go into Bithynia: but the Spirit suffered them not.
> 8 And they passing by Mysia came down to Troas. (Acts 16)

Then he reported the following night vision: "There stood a man of Macedonia, and prayed him, saying, Come over into Macedonia, and help us." (Acts 16:9) Who was this "man of Macedonia?" At first, it seems that Paul saw a man in Macedonia who was praying, asking that Paul come to them. This is not the case. How would a man who has never heard of Paul know to pray for him to come? The man was not praying in the modern sense of the word (praying to heaven), but was urging or asking Paul directly. This "man of Macedonia" was the chief angel over Macedonia. God, knowing Paul was available, allowed that angel to request that he come to Macedonia to help the angels laboring there. Many times we think that the angels exist to help us, and many times that is true. However, there is no reason that we cannot also help them.

There are certain things we can't do without the assistance of angels, and there are certain things angels cannot do without our help. If we are going to interact in the spirit realm, we must understand the hierarchy that exists there. Just as regions have chief angels and all ranks of subordinate angels, regions have chief demons and all ranks of subordinate demons. Just as angels interact with demons and men, demons interact with angels and men. When righteous Daniel prayed for understanding, God dispatched Gabriel to answer his prayer. Mighty Gabriel was detained by the demonic chief angel over Persia.

> 12 Then said he unto me, Fear not, Daniel: for from the first day that thou didst set thine heart to understand, and to chasten thyself before thy God, thy words were heard, and I am come for thy words.
> 13 But the prince of the kingdom of Persia withstood me one and twenty days: but, lo, Michael, one of the chief princes, came to help me; and I remained there with the kings of Persia. (Daniel 10:12-13)

This demonic prince was so powerful that Gabriel was unable to conquer him until the archangel Michael came to assist him.

Some Christians foolishly assume that they have authority over all demons, or that they as humans are mightier than all angels. There is no scripture that suggests that such is the case. In fact, there is ample evidence to the contrary. Despite Daniel's righteousness, when Gabriel appeared to him he collapsed from the strain of being in Gabriel's presence. Yet, Gabriel is lower in glory than Michael, whose extra strength was required to overcome the prince of Persia. Though Michael is capable of overcoming chief demons, for now he must rely on the Lord to rebuke Satan himself (see Jude 1:9). To think that somehow a normal man can have authority over Satan when Daniel, Gabriel, and Michael cannot is great folly. Satan and many of his minions have greater authority than the typical man.

When demons are rebuked by men they outrank, the demons laugh at their ignorance. They are apt to physically harm those who engage them without sufficient authority, as happened to the sons of Sceva:

> 13 Then certain of the vagabond Jews, exorcists, took upon them to call over them which had evil spirits the name of the Lord Jesus, saying, We adjure you by Jesus whom Paul preacheth.
> 14 And there were seven sons of one Sceva, a Jew, and chief of the priests, which did so.
> 15 And the evil spirit answered and said, Jesus I know, and Paul I know; but who are ye?
> 16 And the man in whom the evil spirit was leaped on them, and overcame them, and prevailed against them, so that they fled out of that house naked and wounded. (Acts 19:13-16)

Consider the legion of demons that the Lord cast out of the Gergesene man. The account says that this man occupied tombs that were along a popular road. People had to avoid the road because the man would hurt them. They expended great effort to chain him, but the demons gave him superhuman strength to break the chains. What do you suppose would have happened to the Lord if he had approached this possessed man without sufficient authority to cast out the demons? It is easier to tear apart a man than iron chains!

When you exceed your authority with demons, they will unleash their power on you. This can result in great physical and spiritual harm.

This is why it is very important to understand what power and authority you have with God. Obtaining that power and authority is the subject of the next chapter.

For far too long, Christians have lived below their privileges as our angelic advocates have been underutilized. It is time to become active participants in the decisions of heaven, and to bring to pass God's will on the earth.

Obtaining Power and Authority with God

And Christ hath said: If ye will have faith in me ye shall have power to do whatsoever thing is expedient in me.
(Moroni 7:33)

Most Christians fall into two camps. Either they have settled for a passive but mediocre life that is quite far from the experiences of believers as recorded in scripture, or they live an active but frustrated life, trying and trying but failing to achieve the kind of experiences of believers recorded in scriptures. In both cases, the disconnect is caused by one or both of the following failings: Failure to understand and live repentance (discussed earlier in Part 1), and/or failure to understand and interact with the spirit world. Repentance and movement in the spirit world are absolutely essential to coming to know the Lord. There is no other way.

The failure of Christians to demonstrate the fruits of what they profess to believe drives away atheists and agnostics with greater power than any of Satan's temptations. Once Elijah won many souls to God by demonstrating that God's power was far greater than that of the priests of Ba'al. How many of today's Christians could produce the same outcome? It ought not be so. Echoes of this power and authority reverberate through the lives of all those in the scriptures who served him.

The Lord Jesus has all power here and authority over everything here. Peter came to the point where he was so charged with God's glory that when he walked by the sick, they were healed merely from his shadow touching them. How do you obtain that kind of power from God? Why are today's self-proclaimed servants so impotent?

God's power and authority flow through his kingdom. Many Christians claim citizenship in God's kingdom, but few possess knowledge of his will beyond their understanding of scripture, and even fewer successfully bring that will to pass in the physical world. Of what use are subjects who do not know the will of their king or who lack the power to do it?

Towards the end of his ministry, the Lord asked Peter a provocative question. The exchange gives us insights into what power and authority are and how we can obtain them:

> 15 He saith unto them, But whom say ye that I am?
> 16 And Simon Peter answered and said, Thou art the Christ, the Son of the living God.
> 17 And Jesus answered and said unto him, Blessed art thou, Simon Barjona: for flesh and blood hath not revealed it unto thee, but my Father which is in heaven.
> 18 And I say also unto thee, That thou art Peter, and upon this rock I will build my church; and the gates of hell shall not prevail against it.
> 19 And I will give unto thee the keys of the kingdom of heaven: and whatsoever thou shalt bind on earth shall be bound in heaven: and whatsoever thou shalt loose on earth shall be loosed in heaven.
> 20 Then charged he his disciples that they should tell no man that he was Jesus the Christ. (Matthew 16)

Peter received from Jesus a weighty charge. He received the keys of the kingdom, with the ability to bind on earth and loose on earth. But was the Lord saying that he was only giving these keys to Peter? Many think the answer is yes because this passage uses the singular version of "you"—meaning that the Lord was addressing Peter specifically. Yet, the Lord repeats the same proclamation in Matthew 18 while speaking to his followers in general. There, he uses the plural version of "you," indicating that his charge to Peter was a specific application of what was available generally, not a special charge to Peter. If all followers of Christ have the keys of the kingdom, you do too!

What does it mean to possess the keys of the kingdom? Those who have considered it suppose the keys cause God's power to accompany their works. They have it backwards! The Amplified translation gives us a better understanding:

> I will give you the keys (authority) of the kingdom of heaven; and whatever you bind [forbid, declare to be

111

improper and unlawful] on earth will have [already] been bound in heaven, and whatever you loose [permit, declare lawful] on earth will have [already] been loosed in heaven." (Matthew 16:19, AMP)

Note the order. He was saying, "what is bound in heaven, you bind on earth; what is loosed in heaven, you loose on earth." When the Lord gave the keys of the kingdom to all his followers, what he was giving was the ability to do his will on earth, not to have their will recognized by heaven. This begs the question of how you will know his will.

How do you know what is bound or loosed in heaven? This question is answered in the exchange that spurred this whole conversation. Peter, by revelation from God, declared that the Lord Jesus was the Christ. The Lord responded by saying that revelation was the rock upon which he would build his church. In other words, revelation is the mechanism by which the Lord administers his kingdom. Revelation is how you will know what is bound or loosed in heaven.

Notice that the discussion thus far has been about transmitting on earth what is already decided in heaven. Is this the limit of the charge? No.

As described in this passage and throughout scripture, God's decisions are made in heaven, not on earth. Therefore, if you want to be a participant in that process, you have to effect heavenly councils. If God's power on earth is limited to carrying out what has already been decided in heaven, it also means that you must work in heaven if you are to participate in that decision making process.

What are the keys to the kingdom? They consist in understanding that God's authority operates on earth through his word revealed from and decided upon in heaven. When God gives you the keys to the kingdom, he is saying "I enable you to comprehend the operations and works of my kingdom in heaven, to participate in the decisions that are made there, and to carry out those decisions on earth." There are three charges here: 1) learn what is decided in heaven; 2) do what is decided in heaven on earth; 3) influence what happens in heaven.

1 - Learn what is decided in heaven. The keys to the kingdom are at once an astounding dispensation of power and an incredible check on that power. God does not give his authority to men. Instead, he allows them to act on his authority only when they learn and execute exactly what he wants to be done, how he wants it to be done, when he wants it to be done. Men never have the ability to use God's power autonomously from God. Therefore, learning what he wants to be done, how he wants it to be done, and when he wants it to be done are absolutely essential for all who want to be active subjects in his kingdom.

The essence of the Lord's prayer is "Thy kingdom come, Thy will be done in earth, as it is in heaven." (Matthew 6:10) The only way to learn God's will is through God's word.

Where are we to find God's word? The answer, of course, is revelation.

But what about scripture? Some would suppose that we know everything we need to know about God's will from the scriptures. God's word is certainly found in the scriptures. However, scripture in and of itself is insufficient to teach you God's word.

If the scriptures are the limit of your understanding of what is decided in heaven, you are an ineffective servant of God for two reasons. First, your understanding of what is in the Bible is likely clouded by the false traditions of men. Think of how many different religions claim to be the one and only correct interpretation of the same Bible. Peter wrote that scriptures are understood correctly only when God's original meaning is known: "Knowing this first, that no prophecy of the scripture is of any private interpretation." (2 Peter 1:20) It is not enough to "read the Bible literally," as most Christian sects claim to do, despite their numerous disagreements. Don't you realize that Satan was quoting scripture when he quoted it to the Lord in attempting to convince Jesus to sin? If the Bible can be used by Satan to tempt the righteous to sin, can't it be used to teach false principles?

The Bible was never meant to stand independent of the revelation required to understand it and specifically apply it to your specific circumstances. The only way you can know whether your understanding of scripture is based on private interpretation or God's original intent is if he communicates to you directly. This is revelation.

When you operate without revelation, your instructions are limited to those general instructions found in the scriptures. With only the scriptures, you are like a commando in battle with only the military handbook for guidance. If you expect to benefit from the power wielded by your superiors (air support, ground support, supplies, etc.) and to work in conjunction with your fellow soldiers, you must have a radio where specific communication can flow back and forth between you, your commander, and your fellow units. Revelation provides the two-way communication between you, the Lord, and the angels. It is how the spiritual battle is coordinated. Don't cut yourself off from that channel. Seek it, develop it, and trust it.

The Lord Jesus had the task, as we do, of preaching the acceptable year of the Lord. This cryptic phrase is clarified in the Amplified translation:

> 18 The Spirit of the Lord is upon Me (the Messiah), because He has anointed Me to preach the good news to the poor. He has sent Me to announce release (pardon, forgiveness) to the captives, and recovery of sight to the blind, to set free those who are oppressed (downtrodden, bruised, crushed by tragedy),
> 19 To proclaim the favorable year of the Lord [the day when salvation and the favor of God abound greatly]. (Luke 4, AMP)

The acceptable year of the Lord is a period when salvation and the favor of God abound greatly. The Lord Jesus came to save mankind, but that is not all. He came to pour out the favor of God greatly, demonstrated by his working miracles. Though we cannot work out salvation for others, we are charged to emulate the miraculous works of the Savior, and even charged to do more than he did (see John 14:12).

When we achieve a habitation with God, all things are possible. The Lord promised that those who follow him will do greater things than he did. Yet, what Christian do you know that does even equal to what the Lord Jesus did? A habitation with God is the missing piece of the puzzle.

The Lord was shown exactly what miracles he should work, how he should work them, and when he should work them (see John 5:19). He did not freelance. If the Lord needed specific, special revelation to inform him of his Father's will for the miracles he would do every day, how can we expect to do even more than he did having only the general counsel provided by the scriptures?

The Lord was able to do what he did because he had a habitation with the Father. He said he only did those things that his Father showed him to do. You cannot achieve that kind of power of God in your life without a habitation with God, so he can tell you what to do every day. You have to know his will to do his works, and you have to know him in order to know his will.

2 - Do what is decided in heaven on earth. Most Christians live only in this aspect of the keys, and even this they do only partially. They are confined to action in the physical realm, with only a partial or sometimes even incorrect understanding of what is decided in heaven. God's miraculous works require faith.

While you can believe in anything you choose, God is only found in what is true. You cannot have faith in something that is not true. Therefore, your capacity to execute the power of God is limited to your understanding of the decisions made in heaven. You will never encounter God's power while doing something that is contrary to the will of heaven. This is one reason the lives of most Christians are devoid of tangible manifestations of God's power: they do not know God's will for them, and are merely guessing what it might be.

Some manage to muster sufficient belief to make great sacrifices and then wonder why they fail to connect with God in spite of great cost. Most will not engage in the risky, embarrassing, or difficult tasks God requires if they are merely guessing that they are God's will. Yet, God's power seems to be largely confined to precisely those types of situations. The famous stories from scripture did not take place when someone was sitting at home on their couch watching TV. Instead, the people involved were risking their lives, their wealth, and their comfort in actively carrying out God's will as revealed specifically to them.

You cannot do on earth what is decided in heaven without knowledge of what is decided in heaven. You can't put yourself into artificially difficult situations and experience the same relationship with God as those whose trials are sanctioned by heaven.

Many Christians erroneously believe that God gives his authority to men. Working mighty works in God is not a result of him having given to you some special authority that no one else has. Instead, he gives his word to an individual (sometimes following a prayerful request), dictating precisely what they should do, how they should do it, and when they should do it. God told Moses to part the Red Sea. He told him how to do it. God told Elijah to call down fire from heaven. Elijah was given specific instructions, including to dig a ditch around the altar and pour enough water on the sacrifice to fill the ditch.

God does not give his power to men. He said:

1 I am the true vine, and my Father is the husbandman.

2 Every branch in me that beareth not fruit he taketh away: and every branch that beareth fruit, he purgeth it, that it may bring forth more fruit.

3 Now ye are clean through the word which I have spoken unto you.

4 Abide in me, and I in you. *As the branch cannot bear fruit of itself, except it abide in the vine; no more can ye, except ye abide in me.*

5 I am the vine, ye are the branches: He that abideth in me, and I in him, the same bringeth forth much fruit: for *without me ye can do nothing.* (John 15)

Servants of God are not independent agents who can wield God's power without God being involved. Instead, they are always tethered by God's will—and not just in the efficacy of their works. A branch cannot produce fruit independent of the vine. All fruit it produces comes from the vine through the branch. Likewise, men can exercise God's power only if they are connected to God.

True servants of God do not act without having received their mission from God. True servants of God do not give blessings that do not come to pass, prophecies that are not fulfilled, or attempt miracles that do not succeed. This only happens when men freelance.

If you want to do more miraculous works, you need to have God speak to you more often and invite you to do those things. How is this done? You need to repent of all of your sins. You need to hunger and thirst after him. You need to develop the humility, reverence, and trust to do anything he asks you to.

The Lord wants us to talk to him all day. He wants us to include him in our lives. We are told to "pray in the Spirit on all occasions with all kinds of prayers and requests..." (Ephesians 6:18, NIV) We are to pray over the events of the day and our temporal concerns:

19 Yea, humble yourselves, and continue in prayer unto him.

20 Cry unto him when ye are in your fields, yea, over all your flocks.

21 Cry unto him in your houses, yea, over all your household, both morning, mid-day, and evening.

22 Yea, cry unto him against the power of your enemies.

23 Yea, cry unto him against the devil, who is an enemy to all righteousness.

116

24 Cry unto him over the crops of your fields, that ye may prosper in them.

25 Cry over the flocks of your fields, that they may increase.

26 But this is not all; ye must pour out your souls in your closets, and your secret places, and in your wilderness.

27 Yea, and when you do not cry unto the Lord, let your hearts be full, drawn out in prayer unto him continually for your welfare, and also for the welfare of those who are around you. (Alma 34)

If we do this, he will give us instructions for how to carry out our day-to-day lives: "In all thy ways acknowledge him, and he shall direct thy paths." (Proverbs 3:6) When we are on the Lord's errand, we will see the Lord's power. If you want God to exert his power in your life, you have to seek his will in all things.

> But behold, I say unto you that ye must pray always, and not faint; that ye must not perform any thing unto the Lord save in the first place ye shall pray unto the Father in the name of Christ, that he will consecrate thy performance unto thee, that thy performance may be for the welfare of thy soul. (2 Nephi 32:9)

Before you make any decision, check in with him. It doesn't have to be an hour long prayer, just check in. You'll be surprised how many instructions you get. It is very hard for you to get to the place where he will tell you everything about a day in your morning prayer, but it is very easy to stop throughout your day and ask him if he has anything to say about it.

We expect God's miracles to happen in abstract of our normal lives. It doesn't work that way. Consider any miraculous story you've heard. What were the circumstances? It always happens in conjunction with life, not in abstract of it. The separation between our spiritual and temporal lives is artificial and of our own creation, not God's.

There is great peace in aligning your life with the Lord. This is how his yoke becomes easy and his burden light. Imagine if you could turn to God in every difficulty you encounter, knowing that you are doing his perfect will for you. It isn't that trials go away, but that when you love him and align your life to him, you achieve a restful trust in

God, knowing that he is with you and whatever happens is for your good.

> And we know that all things work together for good to them that love God, to them who are the called according to his purpose. (Romans 8:28)

Imagine if you had perfect confidence that God was with you and that everything that happens in your life is for your good. Then, like the Lord Jesus, you could respond to trials knowing God would send 72,000 angels if you asked him to (see Matthew 26:53). We should include him in every aspect of our lives where we want to see his glory work for our good.

When you walk with God, you have an acute awareness of what he is doing in and around you. You don't just believe he is in control, you know he is in control. This was the confidence Paul had. Despite knowing he would be shipwrecked, he had total peace because an angel had come and had promised him that no one would die (see Acts 27:22-25). This was also the source of Stephen's confidence. He faced death by stoning in peace because he saw God's throne and had a perfect knowledge of his goodness and glory, and that God was in control (see Acts 7:55-60). You can't go and do your own thing and then complain that God is not in your life. Filter everything in your life through God, and make every adjustment he suggests. That's how you walk with God and encounter the blessings promised to the faithful.

3 – Influence what happens in heaven. Great miracles are possible when you develop the ability for God to speak to you and inform you of his will, then you perform it here on earth. And yet, that posture is still very passive compared to the fullness of opportunities God provides. The pinnacle of our relationship with God is to come up to the point where he allows us to influence his decisions.

When we include him in our lives, he will start to include us in his. "Draw nigh to God, and he will draw nigh to you..." (James 4:8) This is how we become a friend of God. God counsels with his friends. God shares his secrets with his friends.

> Henceforth I call you not servants; for the servant knoweth not what his lord doeth: but I have called you friends; for all things that I have heard of my Father I have made known unto you. (John 15:15)

118

We tend to think of prophets as being an elite group of people. In reality, they are merely people who accepted the invitation to draw near to God, make him a part of their every day lives, and were obedient to what God told them. "Surely the Lord God will do nothing, but he revealeth his secret unto his servants the prophets." (Amos 3:7)

Abraham was a friend of God. He said: "And the Lord said, Shall I hide from Abraham that thing which I do?" (Genesis 18:17) Before God destroyed Sodom and Gomorrah, he talked it over with Abraham. Abraham was given the opportunity to play an active role in the outcome of the situation. Imagine a city whose survival or destruction depended to a great extent on what you said or did about it. Does that seem far-fetched? Yet, that is exactly the situation you are in. James said that "the effectual fervent prayer of a righteous man availeth much." (James 5:16) Through your righteous life and powerful prayer, you can have just as much effect on the decisions in heaven as Abraham did.

We are too willing to settle for a passive, mediocre existence in God's kingdom. Why wouldn't God use you? Where has he said that only some people can do mighty works for him?

> 27 Wherefore, my beloved brethren, have miracles ceased because Christ hath ascended into heaven, and hath sat down on the right hand of God, to claim of the Father his rights of mercy which he hath upon the children of men?
>
> 37 Behold I say unto you, Nay; for it is by faith that miracles are wrought; and it is by faith that angels appear and minister unto men; wherefore, if these things have ceased wo be unto the children of men, for it is because of unbelief, and all is vain.
>
> 38 For no man can be saved, according to the words of Christ, save they shall have faith in his name; wherefore, if these things have ceased, then has faith ceased also; and awful is the state of man, for they are as though there had been no redemption made. (Moroni 7)

If you lack miracles and mighty works in your life, it is not because God wills it to be so. Rather, it is the outward manifestation of your lack of faith, and without sufficient faith to work mighty miracles, you can rest assured that you do not have sufficient faith to be saved. They always go hand in hand.

We tend to think that our capability is a limiting factor in the good we can do for God. Doing mighty works for God is not a factor of your greatness. The only qualification for mighty works in God is repentance and faith.

Faith. Do you believe that God is all powerful, that you can truly do anything he commands you to do, and that he can command you to do anything?

> And I said unto them: If God had commanded me to do all things I could do them. If he should command me that I should say unto this water, be thou earth, it should be earth; and if I should say it, it would be done. (1 Nephi 17:50)

There was nothing special about Nephi that made his action effectual, except for the fact that God had told him to do it. Will you do anything God tells you?

All men are commanded to repent and have faith. As often as they do, God uses them in marvelous ways.

Do you truly believe you are a fool before God? When we trust in ourselves, we are limited to what we can do of ourselves. When we trust in God, we can do all things through him. "I can do all things through Christ which strengtheneth me." (Phillipians 4:13) Do not underestimate the opportunities to serve God that you are passing by through clinging to confidence in yourself instead of clinging to God. Those who repent and exercise faith can do many great things:

> Yea, he that repenteth and exerciseth faith, and bringeth forth good works, and prayeth continually without ceasing—unto such it is given to know the mysteries of God; yea, unto such it shall be given to reveal things which never have been revealed; yea, and it shall be given unto such to bring thousands of souls to repentance, even as it has been given unto us to bring these our brethren to repentance. (Alma 26:22)

Isaiah's ministry came not through God appointing it to him, but because God showed him a need that he had, and Isaiah—trusting in God's ability to empower him to fulfill it—volunteered to do so: "Also I heard the voice of the Lord, saying, Whom shall I send, and who will go for us? Then said I, Here am I; send me." (Isaiah 6:8)

Isaiah's calling came because he was willing to believe that God could make him capable of preaching repentance to Israel when God told him it needed to happen.

Mighty Moses was a nobody when God called him to lead out Israel. He had gone from being a prince in the mightiest kingdom on earth to being an old servant shepherd (an abomination in the Egyptian culture he was raised in) in a foreign land. Yet, because he was willing to trust in and submit to God, God made him mighty.

Joshua, knowing that God was no respecter of persons, believed that if God would appear to Moses, he would appear to Joshua. He followed Moses' example, and obtained the same result.

Repentance. Are there sins you are aware of that you have not yet changed? You cannot do mighty works of God if you are living in willful sin: "...there was not any man who could do a miracle in the name of Jesus save he were cleansed every whit from his iniquity." (3 Nephi 8:1)

What are you willing to give up for God? Are you totally surrendered? Will you avoid seeking and accepting things that are not God's will to give you? How much time and effort are you willing to spend to know God?

We can gain great power from God if we will admit our nothingness before him. Paul said:

> Let no man deceive himself. If any man among you seemeth to be wise in this world, let him become a fool, that he may be wise. (1 Corinthians 3:18)

When we admit our weakness, he can make us strong.

> 27 And if men come unto me I will show unto them their weakness. I give unto men weakness that they may be humble; and my grace is sufficient for all men that humble themselves before me; for if they humble themselves before me, and have faith in me, then will I make weak things become strong unto them. (Ether 12:27)

You are nothing, but with God you can do anything.

Line Upon Line

For behold, thus saith the Lord God: I will give unto the children of men line upon line, precept upon precept, here a little and there a little; and blessed are those who hearken unto my precepts, and lend an ear unto my counsel, for they shall learn wisdom; for unto him that receiveth I will give more; and from them that shall say, We have enough, from them shall be taken away even that which they have. (2 Nephi 28:30)

Knowing God is not binary. Just as you can know a person a little or a lot, knowledge of God accumulates by degrees: "But the path of the just is as the shining light, that shineth more and more unto the perfect day." (Proverbs 4:18) To truly know God, it is necessary to come to the perfect day, or the point where you have a habitation with him—a constant and consistent seeing and hearing relationship with him. How do you get to this point?

We acquire a habitation with God by keeping the commandments that we have already received. Those who love God keep his commandments: "If ye love me, keep my commandments." (John 14:15) Those who love him and keep his commandments will receive a habitation with God: "...If a man love me, he will keep my words: and my Father will love him, and we will come unto him, and make our abode with him." (John 14:23) "If ye keep my commandments, ye shall abide in my love; even as I have kept my Father's commandments, and abide in his love." (John 15:10)

What does it mean to keep God's commandments? This was the question of a certain man to Jesus. He approached the Lord and asked, "what shall I do to inherit eternal life?" Jesus replied, "Thou knowest the commandments, Do not commit adultery, Do not kill, Do not steal,

Do not bear false witness, Honour thy father and thy mother." The young man considered these to be all the commandments he had to worry about. He said, "All these have I kept from my youth up." He thought he was keeping God's commandments since he was keeping all the commandments he knew. Jesus replied, "Yet lackest thou one thing: sell all that thou hast, and distribute unto the poor, and thou shalt have treasure in heaven: and come, follow me." This was a new commandment for the young man.

Whenever we have complied with the commandments we have received, we ought to expect God to give us more. Those who are faithful to the commandments and knowledge they have received will receive more commandments and knowledge.

> For whomever the Lord Jehovah loves, he instructs, and draws aside his children with whom he is pleased. (Hebrews 12:6, Aramaic Bible)

The young man was not pleased with Jesus' instruction. "And when he heard this, he was very sorrowful: for he was very rich." This was not a specific, once-off instruction to the young man. Jesus continued, "How hardly shall they that have riches enter into the kingdom of God!" (Luke 18:18, 20-24)

This episode shows clearly that not all of God's commandments required to dwell with God are publicly known. Despite being a faithful adherent to God, this young man had no idea that God expected him to rid himself of his riches to qualify for heaven.

It is possible to be forgiven of your sins without knowing the critical mass of commandments required to dwell with God, but it is not possible to dwell in his presence without them. The Father dwells in inapproachable light (see 1 Timothy 6:16). Light, truth, and glory all refer to the goodness of God, and are interchangeable with knowledge. When we say knowledge, we do not mean facts or figures. Instead, we mean spiritual knowledge. A habitation with God comes through incremental increases in light and truth, or knowledge. The glory a person possesses is a function of the character they possess. God gives us commandments to draw us closer to him, to change our character from a lower state to a higher state.

> And behold, I have given you the law and the commandments of my Father, that ye shall believe in me,

124

and that ye shall repent of your sins, and come unto me
with a broken heart and a contrite spirit. (3 Nephi 12:19)

We know God to the extent that we can see and endure his glory.
Although the Father dwells in unapproachable light, the Son can appear
as he chooses—with no glory (as he did on the road to Emmaus), with
all his glory, or anything in between. The glory we can endure is
proportional to the glory that we possess.

Beloved, now are we the sons of God, and it doth not
yet appear what we shall be: but we know that, when he
shall appear, we shall be like him; for we shall see him as
he is. (1 John 3:2)

Salvation is, in reality, a matter of the acquisition of glory through
acquiring and obeying greater light and truth, or greater commandments
and knowledge from God.

How are these higher commandments obtained? God provides
us with new truth as soon as we are ready to receive it. The way he
prepares us for that which we cannot currently bear is by giving us lesser
law that we can bear. He cannot give us greater light and truth until we
comply with what we already have.

9 And now Alma began to expound these things unto
him, saying: It is given unto many to know the mysteries
of God; nevertheless they are laid under a strict
command that they shall not impart only according to
the portion of his word which he doth grant unto the
children of men, according to the heed and diligence
which they give unto him.
10 And therefore, he that will harden his heart, the same
receiveth the lesser portion of the word; and he that will
not harden his heart, to him is given the greater portion
of the word, until it is given unto him to know the
mysteries of God until he know them in full.
11 And they that will harden their hearts, to them is
given the lesser portion of the word until they know
nothing concerning his mysteries; and then they are
taken captive by the devil, and led by his will down to

destruction. Now this is what is meant by the chains of hell. (Alma 12:9-11)

God will patiently send you experiences to build your capacity for obedience until you are capable of keeping higher commandments. He will send them as fast as you are able to keep them, and you will be able to keep them commensurate with your faithfulness to God under all circumstances. Once we are perfectly obedient to what we have received, God will give us more.

New commandments aren't always cleanly separated from what we already know. There are three forms of new truth:

New truth in a new area. This is what most of us think of when we think of new truth. This is where you learn something that you had never before considered.

New truth that expands an area you already know something about. This is where you learn a deeper aspect of something you already knew.

New truth that replaces some currently held belief. This is the least considered and hardest to accept. We tend to think that if we have a witness of a truth, or have seen positive fruits from it, there is no possibility that another perspective on the same issue could be more correct. Spiritual law, like natural law, is progressive. In science, a theory's ability to explain past observations does not guarantee it can explain all future observations. This is just as much the case in spiritual matters. In fact, spiritual truths might be *more* likely to be superseded by higher truth, given that religions tend to deteriorate. For example, the Lord Jesus not only taught the Pharisees truths higher *than* the law of Moses, but he also corrected the tradition-inspired incorrect principles taught *as* the law of Moses. God can reveal truth, and he can reveal higher truth. The Pharisees refused to receive higher truth, and as a result ended up more wicked than if they had never met Jesus.

> For unto every one that hath shall be given, and he shall have abundance: but from him that hath not shall be taken away even that which he hath. (Matthew 25:29)

We should not make the same mistake. We must be willing to let go of what we currently view as true, or even sacrosanct, in order to progress with God. We must be willing to accept his instruction, correction, and reproof.

4 Incline not my heart to any evil thing, to practise wicked works with men that work iniquity: and let me not eat of their dainties.

5 Let the righteous smite me; it shall be a kindness: and *let him reprove me;* it shall be an excellent oil, which shall not break my head: for yet my prayer also shall be in their calamities. (Psalm 141:5)

Where does new truth come from? Paul said:

14 How then shall they call on him in whom they have not believed? and how shall they believe in him of whom they have not heard? and how shall they hear without a preacher?

17 So then faith cometh by hearing, and hearing by the word of God. (Romans 10:14, 17)

We receive new truth from God's word, which comes through direct revelation, from messengers of God, and from indirect experience. Direct revelation occurs when God communicates directly with us. His word may come in the form of a vision, a visitation, or a voice. These messages can come in expected settings, like when we are praying or reading the scriptures. They can also come in unexpected settings. You can have visions while sleeping, an angel could visit you while you are at work, or you could hear the voice of God while on errands. When we are observant of the world around us, and spend ample time in reflective meditation, we open the doors for the Lord to teach us new truth. Seemingly normal experiences in nature, at work, or in our homes can trigger an opportunity to learn deep truth.

Messengers from God can be either heavenly or human. If the message they carry is the word of God, it carries the same weight no matter if it is delivered by a man, an angel, the Holy Ghost, or the Lord himself. Some disregard the possibility that God might send them new truth through imperfect humans. These would do well to reread the scriptures, where God's messengers were commonly the only voice of warning the public received before gross destruction.

The existence of human messengers does not imply that all who claim to have a message from God actually do. Every message must be independently evaluated: "...test everything; hold fast what is good." (1

Thessalonians 5:21) One part of a sermon can be correct, even if another is not.

Every channel of new truth is counterfeited by the devil. His objective is to keep men as uninstructed as possible. He does this through several means. One way is by convincing men to reject anything that contradicts what they already believe instead of doing as God said, investigating the fruits of the new knowledge. Another way is by convincing them not to seek out higher truth. Another way is to flood the world with truth mixed with error. This manifests in many ways, including cult following of certain religious leaders, who gradually mix in more and more error to what were once reasonably enlightening teachings. The inevitable outcome of such situations is that some residue of what was once an extensive following become sycophants to an obviously false cause, publicly reducing the faith of men in the possibility of true messengers and true religion. The devil ensures that for every true signal, there are many false ones.

With the stakes so high, how do we recognize what is true and what is false? It is not as simple as comparing everything to the scriptures. The scriptures contain God's word, but our capacity to read them literally and as they were intended is limited by the constant flood of traditions we are exposed to, many of which are false.

The task of discerning truth is difficult. Because the gospel is progressive, we cannot simply have a static list of all of God's commandments. Though many commandments will be common to many personal lists, God will give each of us individualized instructions suited for our situation. In this fluid situation, a custom, individual mechanism for evaluating truth is required, and that is exactly what God has given us.

God has given each of us a spirit capable of discerning truth from error.

> 15 For behold, my brethren, it is given unto you to judge, that ye may know good from evil; and the way to judge is as plain, that ye may know with a perfect knowledge, as the daylight is from the dark night.
> 16 For behold, the Spirit of Christ is given to every man, that he may know good from evil... (Moroni 7)

The Lord taught that this discernment is not corporal, but spiritual: "Judge not according to the appearance, but judge righteous judgment."

(John 7:24) If we seek God, he will teach us the truthfulness of each message: "And by the power of the Holy Ghost ye may know the truth of all things." (Moroni 10:5) The Holy Ghost is the key arbiter in our search for truth. He will show us everything we should do:

> For behold, again I say unto you that if ye will enter in by the way, and receive the Holy Ghost, it will show unto you all things what ye should do. (2 Nephi 32:5)

Have you ever attended a sermon where you came away having learned something that the speaker did not mention? If so, you have received ample evidence that, while God uses messengers and experiences to teach his children, he never fully lets go of the reins. God never expects any of us to believe anything we hear from any source without an independent confirmation through that portion of his spirit that resides in us. This is how we detect things that are not true, as well as any additional truth beyond the content of the message in the form delivered.

Since specifics depend on the individual's state and circumstance, guidelines to discern between truth and evil have to be generally defined. Paul said:

> … whatsoever things are true, whatsoever things are honest, whatsoever things are just, whatsoever things are pure, whatsoever things are lovely, whatsoever things are of good report; if there be any virtue, and if there be any praise, think on these things. (Philippians 4:8)

Moroni also described the difference in terms of good and evil, clarifying the difference:

> 12 Wherefore, all things which are good cometh of God; and that which is evil cometh of the devil; for the devil is an enemy unto God, and fighteth against him continually, and inviteth and enticeth to sin, and to do that which is evil continually.
> 13 But behold, that which is of God inviteth and enticeth to do good continually; wherefore, every thing which inviteth and enticeth to do good, and to love God, and to serve him, is inspired of God.

16 …every thing which inviteth to do good, and to persuade to believe in Christ, is sent forth by the power and gift of Christ; wherefore ye may know with a perfect knowledge it is of God.

17 But whatsoever thing persuadeth men to do evil, and believe not in Christ, and deny him, and serve not God, then ye may know with a perfect knowledge it is of the devil... (Moroni 7)

In short, anything that draws you closer to God than you currently are is of God.

How do you invite more light and truth into your life? The first way is through recognizing that whatever you think you have, God has more. Your greatest barrier to progression is an inflated perception of your true state with God. Your perception of God's glory is significantly less than the truth. This cannot be helped except through increasing your experiences with him: how much of God's glory you can perceive is limited by how much of his glory you possess. Due to this chronic underestimation of God's greatness, you almost always believe you are more righteous than you actually are.

The young man who came to the Lord and asked him what good thing he could do to gain eternal life thought that he was more righteous than he was (see Matthew 19). His question indicated that he didn't think he had eternal life yet (making him a step ahead of most of us who claim we have it without any evidence that such is the case). His response to Jesus' answer indicates that he didn't anticipate being so far from it as he was. It turns out that his approach was fundamentally flawed. The man thought that salvation could be attained through obeying a laundry list of commandments received through a man: "what good thing shall I do that I may have eternal life?" (Matthew 19:16) He didn't understand that eternal life requires a relationship with God—no one has ever been saved without knowing God, let alone without ever having met him. An interactive relationship with God is a requirement. It is not possible for someone else to access God, get a list of "good things," and pass them onto you. That process places someone else between you and God. The gospel is not a static list. It is a personal, interactive relationship with God. Any list is meant as a teaser to get you to the point where you gain that personal, interactive relationship. It's training wheels. You can't ride to heaven with training wheels.

Despite the failure of this young man to receive new commandments from Jesus, his actions in obtaining more light and truth demonstrate a process that each of us can follow. After asking the Lord what more he could do, the Lord said, "if thou wilt enter into life, keep the commandments." (Matthew 19:17) The man did not deserve further light and truth. He was not ready for it. The Lord, who already knew the next required step in this man's progression, was trying to avoid his question. By divine law, he could not give this man a commandment he was not capable of obeying. He dodged the question while also giving the young man a hint to help him on his way. The man had called Jesus good. Jesus replied, "None is good, save the Father." The Lord—who was the holiest man this or any other person had ever seen—was unwilling to have someone call him good. He was trying to help the man realize that perhaps the man was not as righteous as he thought.

The man tried again. He asked which commandments he should keep. Now, as another clue, Jesus included "Thou shalt love thy neighbor as thyself" among the commandments he listed. This man *thought* he was already obeying this commandment. The truth was that it consisted of far more than he understood. While he should have replied saying, "Oh Jesus, have mercy on me, a sinner," he instead said that he had done all of this since his youth. Instead of approaching the Lord to find out how he could grow, he was looking for justification for his present state. He had filled his life with his dead religious works instead of connection to God. Still, instead of walking away, the young man continued questioning God. His persistence was recognized and rewarded by God.

The loving Lord replied to his persistence with total, blunt instruction:

> Jesus said unto him, If thou wilt be perfect, go and sell that thou hast, and give to the poor, and thou shalt have treasure in heaven: and come and follow me. (Matthew 19:21)

The Lord Jesus always tries to teach things softly at first, and usually doesn't go past that unless we ask him to. Because we don't, we miss most of God's attempts to teach us.

New commandments can't come without increased capacity to obey. Heed and diligence are required to increase our capacity to obey as yet unknown commandments.

Like this man, we ought to persist with God, begging him to be blunt with us in our oblivious ignorance. We ought to plead with God daily to reveal more light and truth to us. He will answer that prayer. He can do this in many ways. He will speak to your mind and your heart. God can send an angel to teach you, or come to you himself. You may hear an audible voice. You may be led to a particular scripture. You may be prompted to investigate certain books or Bible translations. You may be prompted to look at certain videos or websites. You may have a gospel conversation with a new acquaintance or an old friend. It is impossible to list every possibility. Have an open mind.

We can't progress in ignorance. It is better to know of our faults with God rather than incorrectly believe we are righteous. No man is as righteous as God.

We tend to think that we believe in God. And yet, our actions betray our unbelief. If we really believed in God, we would act far differently than we do. When Jesus told the apostles of his impending crucifixion, they said:

> 30 Now are we sure that thou knowest all things, and needest not that any man should ask thee: by this we believe that thou camest forth from God.
> 31 Jesus answered them, Do ye now believe?
> 32 Behold, the hour cometh, yea, is now come, that ye shall be scattered, every man to his own, and shall leave me alone: and yet I am not alone, because the Father is with me. (John 16)

The apostles genuinely thought they were converted, but the Lord knew that they would shortly flee from him. The Lord allowed the apostles to believe all sorts of things that were not exactly correct. If they had just asked him, he would have corrected them. What does he know about you or me? What is he willing to tell us if we just ask?

We ought to welcome challenges to our paradigm. If our theology is not yielding the results of the ancients, our theology is flawed. We ought to pray to God and ask him to correct us, and we ought to expect him to send encounters that help us to reject our false traditions. What better thing could we do to obtain a closer relationship with him than ask him directly how to improve it? Are you ready to accept what he says?

Real Intent

---

*For behold, God hath said a man being evil cannot do
that which is good; for if he offereth a gift, or prayeth
unto God, except he shall do it with real intent it
profiteth him nothing. For behold, it is not counted unto
him for righteousness. For behold, if a man being evil
giveth a gift, he doeth it grudgingly; wherefore it is
counted unto him the same as if he had retained the gift;
wherefore he is counted evil before God. (Moroni 7:6-8)*

Is prayer a chore for you? Do you run out of things to say? Do
you fall asleep when you pray? Does your mind wander?

True prayer is something you desire. Once you have experienced
it, you'll want to pray all the time. It will be difficult *not* to pray when
given the opportunity. It will be difficult not to make the opportunity,
even when it is not readily available. You will wake up early to pray. You
will stay up late to pray. You will sneak prayers in your office at work.
You will see weekends and vacations as a time to get in extra prayers.

Does all of this sound incredible? Is it hard to believe? If so, it
is because you are thinking of *normal* prayer, not true prayer. True prayer,
or correct prayer, is what God means when he uses the word. Normal
prayer is what we do instead.

Like a bow and arrow, prayer is so simple that it can be used by
a small child, yet takes incredible skill to wield with the intended
precision and capability. There is a big difference between a crude bow
and arrow fashioned from a stick and piece of twine and a modern
compound bow. Obtaining superior results from the latter takes
training. So it is with prayer. First you must obtain advanced knowledge,
then you must practice using it until your skills are honed.

What makes true prayer so desirable, and how is it different than
normal prayer? True prayer occurs when there is an active connection

between you and heaven. This connection quickens you with the Holy Ghost. True prayer basks you in the glory of a higher world, every time. True prayer opens the door to visits from heaven and visits to heaven. True prayer tangibly effects every aspect of your life outside of prayer. There is nothing you can do of your own volition that is more important or more beneficial to you than engaging in true prayer. It is your strongest lifeline to God, and yet so little is commonly understood about it.

True prayer brings three types of blessings. The first type are blessings that occur during your prayers every time you pray. Every single time you pray you should connect to heaven. This is the point. If you do not connect to heaven during a prayer, you are doing it wrong and wasting your time. Evil spirits love to tell men not to pray, but they also love when men don't know how to pray. Every normal prayer you offer distances you from God because it trains you to believe that he isn't there, doesn't care, and that prayer doesn't do anything. True prayer creates a connection to heaven, and that conduit channels fire into your soul. It changes your heart, basks you in the love of God, strengthens you against temptation, quickens your mind to receive revelation, and cleans your spiritual eyes from the scales the world darkens them with. This connection consists of—at a minimum—the fire and voice of God's spirit. Every prayer you offer ought to be a two-way communication. You can ask questions and receive answers every time you pray, and you can feel God's love and power every time you pray.

The second type of blessings from true prayer are those that come while you are praying, but may not come every time. These include visits from God, visits from angels, visits to heaven, visions, prophecies, promises from God, mighty miracles, and revelations of mysteries.

The third type of blessings from true prayer are blessings that occur after prayers because of prayers. True prayer touches every aspect of your life. It will subdue the natural man, strengthen your resistance to temptation, make your character more Christ-like, and increase the frequency of spiritual manifestations (visits from God, visits from angels, visits to heaven, visions, prophecies, promises from God, mighty miracles, and revelations of mysteries) throughout your day.

People who struggle to pray struggle because they have yet to experience true prayer. The process of achieving true prayer is described in several chapters in this book. Here, instead of discussing how this is achieved, we will discuss one aspect of what it is like, which can be described as real intent.

The Lord said: "The light of the body is the eye: if therefore thine eye be single, thy whole body shall be full of light." (Matthew 6:22) What do you desire? The Lord said "Blessed are they which do hunger and thirst after righteousness: for they shall be filled." (Matthew 5:6) The Lord fills those who hunger and thirst. A person prays with real intent when they desire the Lord more than anything in this world. In this condition, you are driven to your knees in longing, consummate desire to commune with God.

When you exercise real intent, your prayers become consummate. You rid you mind of all other concerns. You lose track of what you are doing later in the day, what time it is, and even where you are. If you find yourself falling asleep, real intent causes you to pray in the morning and to go to bed earlier. If you find yourself terminating your prayer because of time, real intent drives you to wake up earlier. Real intent causes you to assume that God will appear to you every time you pray, and influences you to create a situation where you would not be rushed to end that visit.

Real intent causes you to pour out your soul.

> *In my distress* I called upon the Lord, and cried unto my God: he heard my voice out of his temple, and my cry came before him, even into his ears. (Psalm 18:6)

Real intent causes you to pray as if your life depended on it. Peter prayed with real intent when, as he was trying to walk on water, he lost faith and began to sink in the turbulent water: "...he cried, saying, Lord, save me." (Matthew 14:30) The disciples prayed with real intent when they woke up the Lord on another occasion as their boat was sinking in a storm. "And his disciples came to him, and awoke him, saying, Lord, save us: we perish." (Matthew 8:25)

God has provided a vivid type of what praying with real intent looks like in sexual intercourse. In fact, one reason God created our sexual characteristics is to teach us about our relationship with him.

> 13 ...Now the body is not for fornication, but for the Lord; and the Lord for the body.
> 16 ...know ye not that he which is joined to an harlot is one body? for two, saith he, shall be one flesh.
> 17 But he that is joined unto the Lord is one spirit. (1 Corinthians 6)

Marital relations teach us to subjugate our body to another entity, in this case a husband or wife. Marriage trains us in what it takes to subjugate our body to God. In our daily, visible, tangible interactions with our spouse, we can learn how to submit our own concerns to the concerns of another. Gradually, we can learn how to do the same with an unseen God whose needs are not as easily discerned as our spouse.

> 3 Let the husband render unto the wife due benevolence: and likewise also the wife unto the husband.
> 4 The wife hath not power of her own body, but the husband: and likewise also the husband hath not power of his own body, but the wife. (2 Corinthians 7)

Good sex requires total, absolute focus. No one stops to scratch an itch. No one stops to talk about an idea that just popped in their heads. There is utter, complete focus. Good sex takes time, and there is a preliminary process to ensure a positive experience. It is not something you can do while thinking only about yourself. In fact, it is most intense when you focus totally on your spouse's desires.

Like sex, good prayer results both in waves of euphoria and a culminating climax of communion—but with God instead of your spouse. This is a concentrated feeling of love in being one with him and being in his presence. Good prayer will drive you to desire more good prayer. As more time passes from the last good prayer, one's desire to experience it again increases.

Sex teaches us how our communion with God matures. At first, an individual pursues sex solely as a way to satisfy their own desires. As they mature, they begin to see that the best sex occurs when both partners are consummately seeking the welfare of the other. If prayer is used for asking for one's desires, this is a cheap substitute for real prayer. God consummately seeks our welfare. When we make prayer a matter of seeking and submitting to his will, and focus our entire being to that end, prayer becomes the immensely positive experience it is meant to be.

Real intent doesn't quit. Knowing God is hard. There is no shortcut. It takes time. Even the Lord, who was perfect, required hours of communion with God per day in order to establish the required connection with his Father. Should we expect to be able to do this in less time being so much less than Jesus?

Many say, "well, I do not have that kind of time." The Lord said, "the care of this world, and the deceitfulness of riches, choke the word, and [makes people] unfruitful." (Matthew 13:22) The cares of the world have far too much control over Christians. When the cares of the world choke off your prayer, choke them back! Every time you turn away from a potential distraction to your prayer, God will recognize it as evidence of your real intent.

> 22 And he said unto his disciples, Therefore I say unto you, Take no thought for your life, what ye shall eat; neither for the body, what ye shall put on.
> 23 The life is more than meat, and the body is more than raiment.
> 24 Consider the ravens: for they neither sow nor reap; which neither have storehouse nor barn; and God feedeth them: how much more are ye better than the fowls?
> 25 And which of you with taking thought can add to his stature one cubit?
> 26 If ye then be not able to do that thing which is least, why take ye thought for the rest?
> 27 Consider the lilies how they grow: they toil not, they spin not; and yet I say unto you, that Solomon in all his glory was not arrayed like one of these.
> 28 If then God so clothe the grass, which is to day in the field, and to morrow is cast into the oven; how much more will he clothe you, O ye of little faith?
> 29 And seek not ye what ye shall eat, or what ye shall drink, neither be ye of doubtful mind.
> 30 For all these things do the nations of the world seek after: and your Father knoweth that ye have need of these things.
> 31 But rather seek ye the kingdom of God; and all these things shall be added unto you. (Luke 12)

Your relationship with God is more important than anything in this world. Don't let the world abort your relationship with God before it is consummated.

When you have real intent, you won't quit praying until your prayer is answered. The Lord taught the parable of the importunate widow to illustrate that we should not give up until our prayers are answered:

> 1 And he spake a parable unto them to this end, that men ought always to pray, and not to faint;
> 2 Saying, There was in a city a judge, which feared not God, neither regarded man:
> 3 And there was a widow in that city; and she came unto him, saying, Avenge me of mine adversary.
> 4 And he would not for a while: but afterward he said within himself, Though I fear not God, nor regard man;
> 5 Yet because this widow troubleth me, I will avenge her, lest by her continual coming she weary me.
> 6 And the Lord said, Hear what the unjust judge saith.
> 7 And shall not God avenge his own elect, which cry day and night unto him, though he bear long with them? (Luke 18)

How long will you have to pray before God grants you what you desire? When God grants you a taste of what is possible, it will be enough to motivate you to try for however long it takes. It could take one quick prayer, several hours of prayer, several days of prayer, and maybe even months or years. There is no set time.

To be successful, you have to be resigned to pray daily with real intent for as long as it takes, even for the rest of your life. When Joshua accompanied Moses into the tabernacle, he would remain behind even after Moses had left:

> 8 And it came to pass, when Moses went out unto the tabernacle, that all the people rose up, and stood every man at his tent door, and looked after Moses, until he was gone into the tabernacle.
> 11 And the Lord spake unto Moses face to face, as a man speaketh unto his friend. And he turned again into the camp: but his servant Joshua, the son of Nun, a young man, departed not out of the tabernacle. (Exodus 33:8,11)

Joshua had real intent in seeking the Lord. You should, too.

The Lord blesses those who persist in seeking him:

6 Who will render to every man according to his deeds:
7 To them who by patient continuance in well doing seek for glory and honour and immortality, eternal life: (Romans 2)

Without real intent, our prayers will never draw us from the cares of the world into the peace and power that a relationship with God can offer. When we practice real intent, we will achieve the kinds of prayers we are meant to have.

Reverence for God

Let us hear the conclusion of the whole matter: Fear God, and keep his commandments: for this is the whole duty of man. (Ecclesiastes 12:13)

When I was in the military, we were taught the protocol to follow when we came into the presence of a superior. We were to stop whatever we were doing and come to attention until told to. Even then, we were to assume a rigid and uncomfortable posture known ironically as "parade rest" until the superior left. You stayed that way for as long as it took. When we expected a visit from even higher authorities, all normal work ceased as everyone turned their attention to making sure the entire environment was transformed into unlivable perfection.

It amazes me how willing we are to modify our behavior for worldly potentates, but how casual we are with God. In the military, you live by the protocol first out of fear of punishment. It is preferable to hurt a little from the protocol than it is to hurt a lot from hundreds of pushups. Eventually, you come to appreciate why it has to be that way. If men are willing to go through such great lengths for fear of men, why are we so unwilling to live by a protocol in our interactions with God? If so much is possible through fear, how much more through love?

God is not petty enough to require that we bow and scrape to him. He is unbelievably willing to condescend and endure much harsher abuse than our disrespectful attitude towards him. His glory does not depend on our willingness or ability to comprehend it. Reverence of him is not for *his* benefit. We are too insignificant to effect his glory one way or the other. Instead, like all other aspects of the gospel, our reverence of him is for *our* benefit. As we realize who he really is, and who we really are, it changes our behavior.

...if ye have known of [God's] goodness and have tasted of his love, and have received a remission of your sins, which causeth such exceedingly great joy in your souls, even so I would that ye should remember, and always retain in remembrance, the greatness of God, and your own nothingness, and his goodness and long-suffering towards you, unworthy creatures, and humble yourselves even in the depths of humility... (Mosiah 4:11)

Did you know that powerful angels, with glory great enough to knock you to the ground were they to appear to you, fall to their faces in reverent worship every time the name of Jesus Christ is mentioned in heaven?

10 And cried with a loud voice, saying, Salvation to our God which sitteth upon the throne, and unto the Lamb. 11 And all the angels stood round about the throne, and about the elders and the four beasts, and fell before the throne on their faces, and worshipped God, 12 Saying, Amen: Blessing, and glory, and wisdom, and thanksgiving, and honour, and power, and might, be unto our God for ever and ever. Amen. (Revelation 7)

Yet, here on earth, many who profess to be his followers refer to him in casual terms, as if he were their gym buddy. The Lord Jesus is the Lion of Judah, the Lamb of God, the Redeemer, the Son of God, the Everlasting Father, the King of Kings, the Lord of Lords. He sits on the throne surrounded by concourses of powerful beings who actively worship him and conduct the government of heaven.

Which of us would casually approach an earthly king? Who would dare approach and converse with a powerful mortal man without great care for what we say? There isn't one of us who would act casually in front of the ruler of a great nation. Yet, we are so casual with God. If you truly believe God is the creator of the earth and heavens, has all power, and has worked out salvation through the sacrifice of Jesus Christ, why would you act any less casually in front of him than even the most powerful man in the world?

When we approach this awesome being in prayer, we ought to pray to him as if we were physically in his presence, in all his glory, seated upon his throne. We ought to kneel before our king. We ought to never approach him in a hurry if it can be helped. We ought to have great reverence for his goodness and glory, and cautiously respect his power. We ought to have great appreciation for his mercy in allowing us to converse with him. We ought to seek a private place, where we will not be interrupted, and where we can pray vocally without thinking about who can hear us. For those with families, this almost always means praying very early in the morning, before anyone else has awoken. This is reverence.

Consider the following prayer that provides a wonderful example of reverence. Here, a righteous man instructed to build closed boats to cross the ocean petitions the Lord to miraculously convert stones into sources of light for the voyage:

> 2 O Lord, thou hast said that we must be encompassed about by the floods. Now behold, O Lord, and do not be angry with thy servant because of his weakness before thee; for we know that thou art holy and dwellest in the heavens, and that we are unworthy before thee; because of the fall our natures have become evil continually; nevertheless, O Lord, thou hast given us a commandment that we must call upon thee, that from thee we may receive according to our desires.
> 3 Behold, O Lord, thou hast smitten us because of our iniquity, and hast driven us forth, and for these many years we have been in the wilderness; nevertheless, thou hast been merciful unto us. O Lord, look upon me in pity, and turn away thine anger from this thy people, and suffer not that they shall go forth across this raging deep in darkness; but behold these things which I have molten out of the rock.
> 4 And I know, O Lord, that thou hast all power, and can do whatsoever thou wilt for the benefit of man; therefore touch these stones, O Lord, with thy finger, and prepare them that they may shine forth in darkness; and they shall shine forth unto us in the vessels which we have prepared, that we may have light while we shall cross the sea.

5 Behold, O Lord, thou canst do this. We know that thou art able to show forth great power, which looks small unto the understanding of men. (Ether 3)

In this example, we see the cautious, godly fear of the petitioner. He does not simply blurt out his request. Though his heart is completely focused on his objective, it is carefully wrapped with sincere expressions of his respect for God. He does not presuppose that he has a right to call on God. He does not presuppose that he can dictate what the Lord does. He acknowledges that his petition's merit comes from the mercy of the Lord, not any entitlement. You can see this petition being appropriate to offer to a king on his throne.

Our reverence for God is an indicator of our faith in God. This is he who created the heavens and the earth. This is he who descended from the highest heaven to the earth, endured the cruelest, crudest treatment from those he came to save, and gave himself as a sacrifice for sin. This is he who is so holy that he dwells in everlasting fire so pure that it is described as unapproachable, yet is so humble and meek that he routinely appears without it. This is he who is so glorious that even the devils must bow the knee and acknowledge him. He is the source of Samson's strength, Moses' power, Elijah's fire, Solomon's wisdom, and Noah's salvation. He can raise the dead, level armies, control the elements, and save souls. He is the Messiah. He is worthy. He is God. Reverence him.

Be Still and Know that I am God

For since the beginning of the world men have not heard,
nor perceived by the ear, neither hath the eye seen, O
God, beside thee, what he hath prepared for him that
waiteth for him. (Isaiah 64:4)

Prayer is meant to connect the supplicant to God in a powerful way. Effectual prayer is an absolute requirement for getting to know God. One reason that many prayers are ineffectual is that they do not overcome the gravitational pull of the body. Prayer is a channel to God in the spirit, not the flesh. While your mind is inclined towards the body, it is essentially impossible to offer an effectual prayer.

How can you know whether you are praying in the spirit or in the body? When you pray, are you aware of your surroundings? Are you aware of your body? Are you aware of the passage of time? Do you worry about all the things that you have to do? Do you hear background music or the last show you watched? Does your mind flood with a remembrance of everything under the sun? These are all signs that your prayer is in the body, not in the spirit.

Prayer in the body is an obstacle to true prayer, but it is not insurmountable. In actuality, transitioning from bodily prayer to spiritual prayer is a process that everyone must learn. As you learn this process, you will be able to transition faster and faster, until you can instantly pray in the spirit. Until then, it will require sustained effort.

The first step in achieving spiritual prayer is to find an appropriate place to pray. We are meant to pray always, but this does not mean that wherever we happen to be is an ideal place to pray. In addition to prayers throughout the day wherever we may be, we should set aside special times and places for intentional prayer in an adequate environment. Like learning to ride a bike using training wheels and a smooth, flat surface, helps you focus on the fundamentals, learning to pray in the spirit is much more attainable if you use an ideal setup to train yourself. The ideal spot for prayer will be private enough that you can speak aloud without any concern of discovery by others. You must find a place where you will not be interrupted no matter what—no phones, no alarms, no external sounds, and no intrusion. These requirements are not arbitrary. Prayer requires incredible focus and sustained concentration. As you work in prayer, you will move closer and closer to your goal, building to a crescendo where a connection with heaven is made. Any distraction will pull you out of this process, and your prayer will end fruitless.

In our modern world, it is very difficult to find such a spot. If you live with others, it is likely that you will have to wake up very early in the morning to create an appropriate environment. Waking up very early in the morning is a sacrifice. It requires that you go to bed much earlier, meaning you go without all the things you typically do at night. Normal prayers are very short. True prayer could go on unceasingly. Once you start to experience true prayer, where you actually come into God's presence, you will find yourself not only requiring more time to pray, but desiring more time to pray.

As you allocate more time for prayer, you may run out of sufficient evening time to counterbalance your early rising, and may have to deal with being tired all day. Some struggle with this, some do not. What I can tell you, as one who acutely feels the effects of sleep deprivation, is that the benefits far outweigh the costs. What good is anything else you do in a day if you do not know God? Like fasting, sleep deprivation is an honest metric of how much you really desire God, as it will effect every aspect of your life.

The next step is to learn how to silence your mind. True prayer requires that the Lord speak to you. He will reply to what you say and, more importantly, he will give you what to say. It takes serious work to obtain the Lord's inspiration, and anything but a clear mind just won't do. Thoughts about work, school, family, or any other concern must be totally silenced. This may seem counterintuitive, as we are taught that prayer is mainly about bringing our concerns to God. This is not true, "…for your Father knoweth what things ye have need of, before ye ask him." (Matthew 6:8) The point of prayer is not to tell God what you need, but for God to effect your desires and soothe your soul. Prayer doesn't change *God*, prayer changes *you*.

As a proof that prayer is meant to change you, consider the meaning of each statement in the Lord's prayer. "After this manner therefore pray ye: Our Father which art in heaven, Hallowed be thy name." *Lord, you are holy and powerful.* "Thy kingdom come. Thy will be done in earth, as it is in heaven." *I submit myself to you and your will.* "Give us this day our daily bread." *Lord, I rely upon you for survival.* "And forgive us our debts, as we forgive our debtors." *Help me forgive others, that I may be forgiven.* "And lead us not into temptation, but deliver us from evil: For thine is the kingdom, and the power, and the glory, for ever. Amen." *I will choose not to succumb to temptation, but to follow you because of your goodness to me in teaching me of your kingdom, power, and glory.* (Matthew 6:9-13)

You must give God a blank slate. In order to quiet your mind, you must completely turn off any music or video in your mind. There is no secret to how to do this, it just takes practice. Whereas finding an ideal spot for prayer can be done in a day, it takes time to learn how to silence your mind. As you pray in your prayer location, first try to clear your mind for 5 minutes. Once you have kept a clear mind for 5 minutes, try 15. Keep doing this until you can keep a clear mind indefinitely.

As you are learning to clear your mind, you should also learn how to keep still. Mental stillness is of limited effect if it is not accompanied by physical stillness. Just as it would be inappropriate to turn on music while in the presence of a king, it is equally inappropriate to fidget, scratch, and so on. Every movement risks breaking your concentration, and many movements will detract from your demonstration of submission and respect towards God.

Remember, one key of true prayer is to act exactly as if you were in the presence of God, because that is your goal. If in the presence of God, you would be so transfixed by his beauty, glory, and goodness, that nothing else would be on your mind. Your body would be frozen in reverence. If you pray and are moving around or wandering in thought, you are not focused enough to pierce through to heaven.

When we think of prayer, we think of speaking to God. Yet, this is only a small part of what true prayer consists of. True prayer also includes silent waiting (sometimes called watching). Though lost to our modern memory, this process would have been familiar to those living in historic monarchies. To gain an audience with a king, it was not uncommon to have to wait silently in the presence of the enthroned king until he acknowledged you. We see this recorded in scripture in Esther:

> 1 Now it came to pass on the third day, that Esther put on her royal apparel, and stood in the inner court of the king's house, over against the king's house: and the king

sat upon his royal throne in the royal house, over against the gate of the house.

2 And it was so, when the king saw Esther the queen standing in the court, that she obtained favour in his sight: and the king held out to Esther the golden sceptre that was in his hand. So Esther drew near, and touched the top of the sceptre.

3 Then said the king unto her, What wilt thou, queen Esther? and what is thy request? it shall be even given thee to the half of the kingdom. (Esther 5)

Esther did not approach or speak to the king until he held out his scepter. She was well aware of the protocol of dealing with a king. We do not know how long she waited there before the king noticed her. In another account, a man is required to wait a full hour before the king responds to him (see Alma 18:14). If the Lord is your king, you ought to wait upon him!

> Behold, as the eyes of servants look unto the hand of their masters, and as the eyes of a maiden unto the hand of her mistress; so our eyes wait upon the Lord our God, until that he have mercy upon us. (Psalm 123:2)

Waiting on the Lord sometimes yields blessings that occur during the process. There are several scriptural examples of God blessing someone who was waiting on him. This includes the appearance of heavenly messengers, hearing the voice of God, or the taking place of some other miracle. However, the most common effect of waiting on the Lord is the turning of the heart towards God. Waiting on God allows his Spirit to work on you and turn your heart towards God. This process sanctifies you and prepares you for more significant experiences with him. It is mostly imperceptible in the moment, but its effects are long-term, cascading, and bountiful.

Interactions with God take time. When Moses ascended mount Sinai, he did not immediately come into God's presence. Instead, he waited on him in prayer for six days. It was only on the seventh day that God spoke to him and brought him into heaven.

> 15 And Moses went up into the mount, and a cloud covered the mount.

16 And the glory of the Lord abode upon mount Sinai, and the cloud covered it six days: and the seventh day he called unto Moses out of the midst of the cloud.

17 And the sight of the glory of the Lord was like devouring fire on the top of the mount in the eyes of the children of Israel.

18 And Moses went into the midst of the cloud, and gat him up into the mount: and Moses was in the mount forty days and forty nights. (Exodus 24)

Moses spent six days on his knees waiting on the Lord. The Lord wanted to see him immediately, but six days of sanctification were required. This teaches us an important lesson on waiting. What would have happened if Moses, upon climbing up the mountain, decided that God's absence meant that he should quit and go back down? What would have happened if he came to that conclusion immediately, after one day of prayer, or after five days?

We should never cease seeking the Lord until we find him, no matter what or how long it takes. Many times it is not just you waiting on the Lord, but the Lord waiting on you.

Moses' six day waiting period teaches us something very important about preparing to enter the presence of the Lord. If the Lord were to appear to you without acclimating you to his presence, you would be consumed. Even if the Lord appears without glory, as he can, you will be overwhelmed. Your immediate reaction will be to say, "it is enough Lord!" as you feel as if you will die. Seeing the Lord is like getting into a very hot bath in cold weather. Your immediate reaction is to immediately retreat after only dipping your toe. A better way is to get into the empty tub, and gradually increase the temperature as the water is running. God builds our capacity to endure his presence by gradually exposing us to him, with ladder-like cascading experiences, whether perceptible or not. After his resurrection, the Lord appeared to two men on the road to Emmaus. He appeared as a normal man, and they did not perceive any glory. When he left, they reflected on how their hearts burned within them. Had these two men not been well accustomed to being in the Lord's presence in his mortality, it is unlikely they would have been able to bear his resurrected presence, even without any glory.

Waiting on the Lord is like a charcoaled log in the woodstove. Though the log may appear cooled, it may spring to life if you crack the door and leave it be. When you first wait on the Lord, it seems like nothing is happening. Don't judge with your natural eyes. Keep praying. Your goal is to pierce through the veil each time you offer your morning prayer. It takes time to do that, both in terms of number of sessions of prayer (as you learn to quiet your mind for longer and longer periods of time) and in each individual session (as you refuse to quit until the fire is lit).

Waiting on God is like boiling water. You can't see what is happening until the water suddenly breaks into a boil. Even if you do not receive any communication, you are still changing. Waiting on God is like walking out of a cold, dark house into a bright, sunny day. The very act of waiting on God makes you more holy, because you are exposing yourself to God's glory.

Don't give up! Our attitude ought to be like Habakkuk's: "I will stand upon my watch, and set me upon the tower, and will watch to see what he will say unto me, and what I shall answer when I am reproved." (Habakkuk 2:1) Sometimes these things just take time.

Patient persistence pays off. Usually, the longer we wait, the greater the blessing.

But why do we need to wait before we perceive God's response? Sometimes, instead of us waiting on God, God is actually waiting on us! Despite the fact that God had commanded Moses to come up to the mount to come into his presence, it took six entire days of waiting upon him to prepare Moses for the experience. God had to wait 6 days for Moses to be sanctified enough that he could visit him.

Why does God wait on us? Sometimes we are not yet focused enough:

> 2 For all those things hath mine hand made, and all those things have been, saith the Lord: but to this man will I look, even to him that is poor and of a contrite spirit, and trembleth at my word. (Isaiah 66:2)

Sometimes we are not yet humble enough:

> Though the Lord be high, yet hath he respect unto the lowly: but the proud he knoweth afar off. (Psalm 138:6)

Sometimes God is waiting until we are ready to obey what he needs to tell or show us. Sometimes there are delays caused by workings in the spirit realm. God's response to Daniel was delayed because of an angelic battle (see Daniel 10:11-13).

Beyond immediate blessings, waiting on the Lord provides blessings after the fact. "I waited patiently for the Lord; and he inclined unto me, and heard my cry." (Psalm 40:1) The way this happens is very similar to what happens when we fast. Although blessings can happen during a fast, fasting also provides enduring blessings after the fact. For example, consider the devil that the twelve disciples could not cast out:

> 27 But Jesus took him by the hand, and lifted him up; and he arose.
> 28 And when he was come into the house, his disciples asked him privately, Why could not we cast him out?
> 29 And he said unto them, This kind can come forth by nothing, but by prayer and fasting. (Mark 9)

The Lord Jesus said that devils of this class could only be cast out through prayer and fasting, but then immediately cast out the devil without praying or fasting. The Lord fasted and prayed very often. When the time came, he had already qualified for this blessing with recent prayer and fasting.

Similarly, waiting on the Lord produces blessings outside of prayer, including frequent revelations, prophecy, and the ability to teach with power and authority:

> But this is not all; they had given themselves to much prayer, and fasting; therefore they had the spirit of prophecy, and the spirit of revelation, and when they taught, they taught with power and authority of God. (Alma 17:3)

Waiting on the Lord prevents you from being tempted: "Watch ye and pray, lest ye enter into temptation. The spirit truly is ready, but the flesh is weak." (Mark 14:38) Waiting on the Lord makes you more humble, meek, submissive, patient, full of love, and long-suffering:

> But that ye would humble yourselves before the Lord, and call on his holy name, and watch and pray continually, that ye may not be tempted above that which ye can bear, and thus be led by the Holy Spirit,

becoming humble, meek, submissive, patient, full of love and all long-suffering; (Alma 13:28)

Waiting on the Lord brings about deliverance:

> Therefore, after Alma having established the church at Sidom, seeing a great check, yea, seeing that the people were checked as to the pride of their hearts, and began to humble themselves before God, and began to assemble themselves together at their sanctuaries to worship God before the altar, watching and praying continually, that they might be delivered from Satan, and from death, and from destruction— (Alma 15:17)

Waiting on the Lord brings peace and power in God. There is a reason that the Lord Jesus spent so much time in prayer during his mortal ministry. As Jesus waited on the Father, the Father's glory recharged his spirit to the point that he could radiate it to the world throughout the day. Our daily experience is one in the body. We find ourselves subjected at all times to the fallen nature of this world. When we wait upon God, we silence the body and cut off the influence of this fallen world. As we wait upon God, we operate in the spirit and connect to a higher level of glory than is found in this world.

If all these benefits were not enough, waiting on God is also a commandment. "Wait on the Lord: be of good courage, and he shall strengthen thine heart: wait, I say, on the Lord." (Psalm 27:14) "Hearken unto this, O Job: stand still, and consider the wondrous works of God." (Job 37:14)

We come to know God through waiting on the Lord: "Be still, and know that I am God: I will be exalted among the heathen, I will be exalted in the earth." (Psalm 46:10)

Worship the Lord

*...Holy, holy, holy, is the Lord of hosts: the whole earth is
full of his glory. (Isaiah 6:3)*

Have you ever felt as if there was a barrier between you and
God? Have you ever knelt for prayer and felt like your prayers weren't
leaving the room? Have you ever felt a total absence of desire to pray?
Have you ever felt overcome with anxiety, grief, or depression?

God has placed within your hands the power to connect with
him at any time, and in any place. Establishing that connection will dispel
darkness, fill you with light, open your spiritual eyes, and give you a sure
knowledge of his existence and his love for you. That power is prayer,
and the principle way to open the connection is through worship.

Worship is a word frequently used, but rarely correctly. The
scriptural words translated into English as worship do not mean to sing
or to dance or to attend church. Rather, they mean to hold someone in
high respect by showing reverence and awe while bowing oneself to the
ground.

Worship is a behavior and an attitude, both confined to prayer.
All worship is prayer, and most effective prayer is worship.

The best example of worship comes from the description of the
behavior of the heavenly hosts. Though their behavior merits an
exhaustive study, for the sake of length, we will analyze just one example
describing what happens in heaven as the Lord Jesus opens the book of
seven seals, beginning the events that comprise God's judgment of this
world. In the first part of this description, we are told that opening this
book requires special power, power that is not present even among the
mighty angels in heaven:

2 And I saw a strong angel proclaiming with a loud voice, Who is worthy to open the book, and to loose the seals thereof?

3 And no man in heaven, nor in earth, neither under the earth, was able to open the book, neither to look thereon.

4 And I wept much, because no man was found worthy to open and to read the book, neither to look thereon. (Revelation 5)

Next, John is told that the Lord Jesus is specially qualified to open the book:

5 And one of the elders saith unto me, Weep not: behold, the Lion of the tribe of Juda, the Root of David, hath prevailed to open the book, and to loose the seven seals thereof.

6 And I beheld, and, lo, in the midst of the throne and of the four beasts, and in the midst of the elders, stood a Lamb as it had been slain, having seven horns and seven eyes, which are the seven Spirits of God sent forth into all the earth.

7 And he came and took the book out of the right hand of him that sat upon the throne. (Revelation 5)

John then sees the reaction of the heavenly hosts:

8 And when he had taken the book, the four beasts and four and twenty elders fell down before the Lamb, having every one of them harps, and golden vials full of odours, which are the prayers of saints.

9 And they sung a new song, saying, Thou art worthy to take the book, and to open the seals thereof: for thou wast slain, and hast redeemed us to God by thy blood out of every kindred, and tongue, and people, and nation;

10 And hast made us unto our God kings and priests: and we shall reign on the earth.

11 And I beheld, and I heard the voice of many angels round about the throne and the beasts and the elders:

153

and the number of them was ten thousand times ten thousand, and thousands of thousands;

12 Saying with a loud voice, Worthy is the Lamb that was slain to receive power, and riches, and wisdom, and strength, and honour, and glory, and blessing.

13 And every creature which is in heaven, and on the earth, and under the earth, and such as are in the sea, and all that are in them, heard I saying, Blessing, and honour, and glory, and power, be unto him that sitteth upon the throne, and unto the Lamb for ever and ever.

14 And the four beasts said, Amen. And the four and twenty elders fell down and worshipped him that liveth for ever and ever. (Revelation 5)

What John sees is the true order of worship. Consider the elements. The posture of the elders is part of their worship. They are not standing or sitting. They fall down before the Lord Jesus. They sing to him. Is this a feel-good hymn? Is the focus the music? No. They don't rehearse canned lyrics. They celebrate his eminent acts in spirit-led praise. And the elders are not alone. They are joined by countless numbers of others in heaven, celebrating the works, goodness, and glory of the Lord Jesus.

Worship is the key to open the connection to God. Real worship is the consummate focus on and enumeration of God's goodness. It is God's goodness—not our own—that provides us the opportunity to be saved. When we praise God, we come up to where he patiently waits for us by focusing on and filling ourselves with his goodness.

Real worship comes from the Holy Ghost:

Likewise the Spirit also helpeth our infirmities: for we know not what we should pray for as we ought: but the Spirit itself maketh intercession for us with groanings which cannot be uttered. (Romans 8:26)

It is difficult to immediately connect with the Holy Ghost in worship. You'll typically have to kick start the process by focusing your mind and heart on the goodness of God, producing your own worship. The glory of God quickens us when we speak of the goodness of God. When you do this, the Holy Ghost will flood you because when your heart focuses completely on God's goodness, your whole body fills with light (see Luke 11:34). You move from a lower state of awareness to a higher state, where your perception begins to be quickened by the Holy Ghost. You'll be given what to say. You then produce the same quality of praise given by the angels of heaven because you speak from the same source. When you achieve this, you will be completely focused on what you are saying, not on what to say. In real time, you will be producing praise as rich and beautiful as anything in the Psalms, but customized to very specific things in your present life. You become lost in it. When you achieve this, you'll notice how real worship is like waking up from sleep as your physical presence fades and is replaced with the brilliant richness of the Spirit.

Worship takes us into a holy place. In the temple, when the high priest entered into the holy of holies, he did so in a cloud of incense. The sweet smelling smoke covered the stench and sight of his imperfection. Our worship of God acts like incense to allow us to enter into the presence of God. When you arrive at the quickened state of worship, and you have praised God with everything that the Holy Ghost has told you to say, you have entered into the holy place where God resides, and you can continue with the rest of your prayer with special access to God.

We ought to include this kind of worship in our prayers. In fact, we ought to begin our prayers with this kind of worship every single time we pray. Praise and worship create heaven-piercing humility. They open the door to access to God. Without worship, prayer runs as smoothly as an engine with no oil. When we worship God in this manner, we take on a fruitful mindset in the rest of our prayer, and truly open a channel to heaven.

A beautiful example of worship is provided by David. David received unique commendation from God, yet we focus so often only on his sin—that while grave in degree, was so rare in frequency that it is the only one we have record of. We would do well to pay more attention to his life, asking ourselves why God commended David's heart as like his own. Read these words from 2 Samuel and consider the accurate picture this king—the most powerful man on the earth at the time—had of the Lord. David began by comparing the Lord's greatness to his own nothingness: "...Who am I, O Lord God? and what is my house, that thou hast brought me hitherto?" He spoke of God's knowledge of things to come and how that was a superhuman trait: "...thou hast spoken also of thy servant's house for a great while to come. And is this the manner of man, O Lord God?" He spoke of God's ability to see a man's heart: "And what can David say more unto thee? for thou, Lord God, knowest thy servant." He spoke of God's character: "For thy word's sake, and according to thine own heart, hast thou done all these great things, to make thy servant know them." He praised the Lord: "Wherefore thou art great, O Lord God: for there is none like thee, neither is there any God beside thee, according to all that we have heard with our ears." He recognized God's care for Israel:

> 23 And what one nation in the earth is like thy people, even like Israel, whom God went to redeem for a people to himself, and to make him a name, and to do for you great things and terrible, for thy land, before thy people, which thou redeemedst to thee from Egypt, from the nations and their gods?
> 24 For thou hast confirmed to thyself thy people Israel to be a people unto thee for ever: and thou, Lord, art become their God. (2 Samuel 7)

It was only after all this praise that David asked for God to bless him. Worship takes us into the presence of God. It is like the incense that covered the high priest when he entered the holy of holies. It is from that place that you can offer prayers and receive answers. When we focus our efforts on worshiping God, and wait to make any requests until after we have entered the holy place, we will achieve efficacy in our prayers—they will become what they are meant to be. Prayer without praise and worship will rarely yield the blessings sought. Prayer with praise and worship rarely fails to yield the blessings sought.

Worshipping God is not a matter of sweet-talking him into doing what you want. Worship fills us with his glory. When we are in that quickened state, we are more in tune with his will, and the Holy Ghost will tell us what to say. It is a tangible, immediate way to supercharge our faith.

Praising God reminds us of just how good, merciful, holy, and just he is. Recounting the characteristics of God can also stir us up to greater trust in God, causing us to recommit ourselves to serve him. The prayer of the repentant elders in Nehemiah provides a rich example of how to enumerate God's goodness. Consider the duration of the worship here. It's a long passage, but you need to read every word to grasp the level of detail and patient listing that Nehemiah gives to God.

Compare the length of praise and reflection of God's goodness to the very brief request made at the end:

> 6 Thou, even thou, art Lord alone; thou hast made heaven, the heaven of heavens, with all their host, the earth, and all things that are therein, the seas, and all that is therein, and thou preservest them all; and the host of heaven worshippeth thee.
>
> 7 Thou art the Lord the God, who didst choose Abram, and broughtest him forth out of Ur of the Chaldees, and gavest him the name of Abraham;
>
> 8 And foundest his heart faithful before thee, and madest a covenant with him to give the land of the Canaanites, the Hittites, the Amorites, and the Perizzites, and the Jebusites, and the Girgashites, to give it, I say, to his seed, and hast performed thy words; for thou art righteous:
>
> 9 And didst see the affliction of our fathers in Egypt, and heardest their cry by the Red sea;
>
> 10 And shewedst signs and wonders upon Pharaoh, and on all his servants, and on all the people of his land: for thou knewest that they dealt proudly against them. So didst thou get thee a name, as it is this day.
>
> 11 And thou didst divide the sea before them, so that they went through the midst of the sea on the dry land; and their persecutors thou threwest into the deeps, as a stone into the mighty waters.
>
> 12 Moreover thou leddest them in the day by a cloudy pillar; and in the night by a pillar of fire, to give them light in the way wherein they should go.
>
> 13 Thou camest down also upon mount Sinai, and spakest with them from heaven, and gavest them right judgments, and true laws, good statutes and commandments:
>
> 14 And madest known unto them thy holy sabbath, and commandedst them precepts, statutes, and laws, by the hand of Moses thy servant:
>
> 15 And gavest them bread from heaven for their hunger, and broughtest forth water for them out of the rock for their thirst, and promisedst them that they should go in

to possess the land which thou hadst sworn to give them.

16 But they and our fathers dealt proudly, and hardened their necks, and hearkened not to thy commandments,

17 And refused to obey, neither were mindful of thy wonders that thou didst among them; but hardened their necks, and in their rebellion appointed a captain to return to their bondage: but thou art a God ready to pardon, gracious and merciful, slow to anger, and of great kindness, and forsookest them not.

18 Yea, when they had made them a molten calf, and said, This is thy God that brought thee up out of Egypt, and had wrought great provocations;

19 Yet thou in thy manifold mercies forsookest them not in the wilderness: the pillar of the cloud departed not from them by day, to lead them in the way; neither the pillar of fire by night, to shew them light, and the way wherein they should go.

20 Thou gavest also thy good spirit to instruct them, and withheldest not thy manna from their mouth, and gavest them water for their thirst.

21 Yea, forty years didst thou sustain them in the wilderness, so that they lacked nothing; their clothes waxed not old, and their feet swelled not.

22 Moreover thou gavest them kingdoms and nations, and didst divide them into corners: so they possessed the land of Sihon, and the land of the king of Heshbon, and the land of Og king of Bashan.

23 Their children also multipliedst thou as the stars of heaven, and broughtest them into the land, concerning which thou hadst promised to their fathers, that they should go in to possess it.

24 So the children went in and possessed the land, and thou subduedst before them the inhabitants of the land, the Canaanites, and gavest them into their hands, with their kings, and the people of the land, that they might do with them as they would.

25 And they took strong cities, and a fat land, and possessed houses full of all goods, well digged, vineyards, and oliveyards, and fruit trees in abundance:

so they did eat, and were filled, and became fat, and delighted themselves in thy great goodness.

26 Nevertheless they were disobedient, and rebelled against thee, and cast thy law behind their backs, and slew thy prophets which testified against them to turn them to thee, and they wrought great provocations.

27 Therefore thou deliveredst them into the hand of their enemies, who vexed them: and in the time of their trouble, when they cried unto thee, thou heardest them from heaven; and according to thy manifold mercies thou gavest them saviours, who saved them out of the hand of their enemies.

28 But after they had rest, they did evil again before thee: therefore leftest thou them in the hand of their enemies, so that they had the dominion over them: yet when they returned, and cried unto thee, thou heardest them from heaven; and many times didst thou deliver them according to thy mercies;

29 And testifiedst against them, that thou mightest bring them again unto thy law: yet they dealt proudly, and hearkened not unto thy commandments, but sinned against thy judgments, (which if a man do, he shall live in them;) and withdrew the shoulder, and hardened their neck, and would not hear.

30 Yet many years didst thou forbear them, and testifiedst against them by thy spirit in thy prophets: yet would they not give ear: therefore gavest thou them into the hand of the people of the lands.

31 Nevertheless for thy great mercies' sake thou didst not utterly consume them, nor forsake them; for thou art a gracious and merciful God.

32 Now therefore, our God, the great, the mighty, and the terrible God, who keepest covenant and mercy, let not all the trouble seem little before thee, that hath come upon us, on our kings, on our princes, and on our priests, and on our prophets, and on our fathers, and on all thy people, since the time of the kings of Assyria unto this day.

33 Howbeit thou art just in all that is brought upon us; for thou hast done right, but we have done wickedly:

34 Neither have our kings, our princes, our priests, nor our fathers, kept thy law, nor hearkened unto thy commandments and thy testimonies, wherewith thou didst testify against them.

35 For they have not served thee in their kingdom, and in thy great goodness that thou gavest them, and in the large and fat land which thou gavest before them, neither turned they from their wicked works.

36 Behold, we are servants this day, and for the land that thou gavest unto our fathers to eat the fruit thereof and the good thereof, behold, we are servants in it:

37 And it yieldeth much increase unto the kings whom thou hast set over us because of our sins: also they have dominion over our bodies, and over our cattle, at their pleasure, and we are in great distress.

38 And because of all this we make a sure covenant, and write it; and our princes, Levites, and priests, seal unto it. (Nehemiah 9)

The act of praise overcomes any fear or doubt we may have, and empowers us to work mighty miracles in God's name.

A wonderful example of how worship overcomes fear is given by Nephi's reaction to his brothers after God commanded them through an angelic visit to do something that seemed impossible. His brothers feared because Laban—a man whose private army far outnumbered Nephi and his company—stood in the way of their objective. Nephi responded with worship for God:

1 And it came to pass that I spake unto my brethren, saying: Let us go up again unto Jerusalem, and let us be faithful in keeping the commandments of the Lord; for behold he is mightier than all the earth, then why not mightier than Laban and his fifty, yea, or even than his tens of thousands?

2 Therefore let us go up; let us be strong like unto Moses; for he truly spake unto the waters of the Red Sea and they divided hither and thither, and our fathers came through, out of captivity, on dry ground, and the armies of Pharaoh did follow and were drowned in the waters of the Red Sea.

> 3 Now behold ye know that this is true; and ye also know that an angel hath spoken unto you; wherefore can ye doubt? Let us go up; the Lord is able to deliver us, even as our fathers, and to destroy Laban, even as the Egyptians. (1 Nephi 4)

This intervention increased their faith sufficiently to persuade them to return to Jerusalem—where many waited to kill them—as the angel had commanded them, in spite of the danger.

Though the scriptures contain many excellent examples of worship, we will add just one more here. This is the prayer that Hannah prayed after the Lord healed her barrenness:

> 1 And Hannah prayed, and said, My heart rejoiceth in the Lord, mine horn is exalted in the Lord: my mouth is enlarged over mine enemies; because I rejoice in thy salvation.
>
> 2 There is none holy as the Lord: for there is none beside thee: neither is there any rock like our God.
>
> 3 Talk no more so exceeding proudly; let not arrogancy come out of your mouth: for the Lord is a God of knowledge, and by him actions are weighed.
>
> 4 The bows of the mighty men are broken, and they that stumbled are girded with strength.
>
> 5 They that were full have hired out themselves for bread; and they that were hungry ceased: so that the barren hath born seven; and she that hath many children is waxed feeble.
>
> 6 The Lord killeth, and maketh alive: he bringeth down to the grave, and bringeth up.
>
> 7 The Lord maketh poor, and maketh rich: he bringeth low, and lifteth up.
>
> 8 He raiseth up the poor out of the dust, and lifteth up the beggar from the dunghill, to set them among princes, and to make them inherit the throne of glory: for the pillars of the earth are the Lord's, and he hath set the world upon them.
>
> 9 He will keep the feet of his saints, and the wicked shall be silent in darkness; for by strength shall no man prevail.

10 The adversaries of the Lord shall be broken to pieces; out of heaven shall he thunder upon them: the Lord shall judge the ends of the earth; and he shall give strength unto his king, and exalt the horn of his anointed. (1 Samuel 2:1-10)

Worshipping God is an art that can be refined over time. As you practice this art, you will notice that you can tap into your inward self to stream out a list of very specific instances of his goodness, mercy, holiness, and justice from the scriptures and from your own life, and that this list will be different every time you pray. The Holy Ghost will give you the words to say to the extent that you can focus on your inner man, and as you channel this through your soul and body in worship to God, the Holy Ghost will quicken your mind and body. This effect will empower you to then transition to the rest of your prayer still remaining in the spirit.

In a sense, your reverence determines your standing with God. Those who revere God as the king and creator of everything, as much when he is unseen as they would if he were seen, are guaranteed eternal life in the highest glory. This is because it is impossible to revere him to the fullest while sinning. These will always submit their flesh to his will. They will always be found in obedience. They will always have a grateful heart full of worship. Because of this, no matter where they are presently in their climb towards God, they will eventually attain eternal life.

Asking and Receiving

Ye ask, and receive not, because ye ask amiss, that ye
may consume it upon your lusts. (James 4:3)

The Lord Jesus is the inheritor of all that the Father has. His express desire is to make us co-heirs with him, "...heirs of God, and joint-heirs with Christ; if so be that we suffer with him, that we may be also glorified together." (Romans 8:17) With an understanding of his design and a recognition of the deficit between what he has and what we have, it is natural for us to seek blessings from him. We are even commanded to do so. The Lord taught:

> 7 Ask, and it shall be given you; seek, and ye shall find; knock, and it shall be opened unto you:
> 8 For every one that asketh receiveth; and he that seeketh findeth; and to him that knocketh it shall be opened.
> 9 Or what man is there of you, whom if his son ask bread, will he give him a stone?
> 10 Or if he ask a fish, will he give him a serpent?
> 11 If ye then, being evil, know how to give good gifts unto your children, how much more shall your Father which is in heaven give good things to them that ask him? (Matthew 7)

God desires to bless us, but we frequently misunderstand the way he will do so. While it is good to pray to God for what things we need, it may surprise you to learn that this is not the principle purpose of prayer. He said that if we seek the kingdom of God, everything we need will be given to us (see Matthew 6:33). God already knows what we need:

7 But when ye pray, use not vain repetitions, as the heathen do: for they think that they shall be heard for their much speaking.

8 Be not ye therefore like unto them: for your Father knoweth what things ye have need of, before ye ask him. (Matthew 6)

If asking for blessings isn't the principle purpose of prayer, what is? It turns out that we can experience incredible growth with God by focusing on communication *with* him rather than asking things *from* him.

Prayer is a tool to ease the information asymmetry between you and God. While most of our prayers focus on the line of communication from us to heaven, it really ought to focus on communication from heaven to us. The purpose of prayer is not about telling God what *we* want, but getting God to tell us what *he* wants.

Many prayers go unanswered because the requester seeks to fulfill their lusts. "Ye ask, and receive not, because ye ask amiss, that ye may consume it upon your lusts." (James 4:3) What is lust? It is not merely sexual desire. Lust is any desire born of the flesh. Lusty prayers are those that contain requests stemming from the flesh. The topic of the prayer does not dictate whether it is a fleshy or spiritual prayer. Even something so apparently spiritual as seeking a vision of heaven could actually be a fleshy prayer if it is done for lustful reasons, such as curiosity. Note the lack of distinction between temporal and spiritual issues in the following instructions on prayer:

18 Yea, cry unto him for mercy; for he is mighty to save.

19 Yea, humble yourselves, and continue in prayer unto him.

20 Cry unto him when ye are in your fields, yea, over all your flocks.

21 Cry unto him in your houses, yea, over all your household, both morning, mid-day, and evening.

22 Yea, cry unto him against the power of your enemies.

23 Yea, cry unto him against the devil, who is an enemy to all righteousness.

24 Cry unto him over the crops of your fields, that ye may prosper in them.

25 Cry over the flocks of your fields, that they may increase.

26 But this is not all; ye must pour out your souls in your closets, and your secret places, and in your wilderness.

27 Yea, and when you do not cry unto the Lord, let your hearts be full, drawn out in prayer unto him continually for your welfare, and also for the welfare of those who are around you. (Alma 34)

You can offer a fleshy prayer concerning matters of the spirit, and a spiritual prayer over temporal concerns. The difference lies in whose will we are seeking.

The Lord Jesus sought the will of the Father, not his own. His entire life demonstrated this. He did only what the Father told him to do (see John 14:24). This pattern holds for all of us. God once blessed one of his servants because he had unceasingly sought God's will and not his own:

4 And thou hast...sought my will, and to keep my commandments.

5 And now, because thou hast done this with such unwearyingness, behold, I will bless thee forever.... (Helaman 10)

This should be our motivation and attitude as well.

In order to offer successful prayers, we ought to exert great effort in seeking God to know what to pray for. This effort usually exceeds what we exert on what we actually pray for. God's will informs what we ask for, because successful prayer asks only what God wants. It informs how we will ask, because obtaining God's will requires deliberate, focused, and often times prolonged effort.

This deliberate, focused, and often prolonged process is sometimes called inquiring of the Lord. Inquiring of the Lord connotes that you are seeking God *until he answers you*. It may take hours or days of sustained prayers, or months or years of regular prayers. Because of this, inquiries to God result in revelation. They result in the receipt of the word of God.

Observe how one man described the process of inquiring of the Lord:

7 For immediately after I had learned these things of you I inquired of the Lord concerning the matter. And the word of the Lord came to me by the power of the Holy Ghost, saying:

8 Listen to the words of Christ, your Redeemer, your Lord and your God. Behold, I came into the world not to call the righteous but sinners to repentance; the whole need no physician, but they that are sick; wherefore, little children are whole, for they are not capable of committing sin; wherefore the curse of Adam is taken from them in me, that it hath no power over them; and the law of circumcision is done away in me. (Moroni 8)

He said the *word* of the Lord came to him. He didn't get *feelings* in response to his inquiry. He received transcribable information. Mormon was able to write out the information that was conveyed. He was able to quote God. God spoke to him like one man speaks to another, through the Holy Ghost.

There are other pitfalls to prayer. Wickedness will hinder our prayers. If you are in willful sin, repent first. The Lord answers the prayers of the wicked more slowly than the righteous. Though it takes extra time, God will eventually respond to the cries of the wicked. It takes time and happens by degrees and only in response to great humility and repentance:

13 And they did humble themselves even to the dust, subjecting themselves to the yoke of bondage, submitting themselves to be smitten, and to be driven to and fro, and burdened, according to the desires of their enemies.

14 And they did humble themselves even in the depths of humility; and they did cry mightily to God; yea, even all the day long did they cry unto their God that he would deliver them out of their afflictions.

15 And now the Lord was slow to hear their cry because of their iniquities; nevertheless the Lord did hear their cries....

16 And...began to prosper [them] by degrees in the land.... (Mosiah 21)

God does not heed the prayers of those who ignore the cry of the poor and needy:

> 7 Should ye not hear the words which the Lord hath cried by the former prophets, when Jerusalem was inhabited and in prosperity, and the cities thereof round about her, when men inhabited the south and the plain?
> 8 And the word of the Lord came unto Zechariah, saying,
> 9 Thus speaketh the Lord of hosts, saying, Execute true judgment, and shew mercy and compassions every man to his brother:
> 10 And oppress not the widow, nor the fatherless, the stranger, nor the poor; and let none of you imagine evil against his brother in your heart.
> 11 But they refused to hearken, and pulled away the shoulder, and stopped their ears, that they should not hear.
> 12 Yea, they made their hearts as an adamant stone, lest they should hear the law, and the words which the Lord of hosts hath sent in his spirit by the former prophets: therefore came a great wrath from the Lord of hosts.
> 13 Therefore it is come to pass, that as he cried, and they would not hear; so they cried, and I would not hear, saith the Lord of hosts: (Zechariah 7)

If you want God to respond to your prayers to him, first make sure you answer the requests of others to you.

Similarly, if you want God to respond to your questions of doctrine, first make sure you have already consulted the words he has revealed to others in the scriptures.

If you want God to forgive you, first forgive others.

To get answers to prayers, care for the poor, fight for the oppressed, and do what God has asked you to do:

> 10 Hear the word of Jehovah, O leaders of Sodom; give heed to the law of our God, you people of Gomorrah!
> 11 For what purpose are your abundant sacrifices to me? says Jehovah. I have had my fill of offerings of rams and

fat of fatted beasts; the blood of bulls and sheep and he-goats I do not want.

12 When you come to see me, who requires you to trample my courts so?

13 Bring no more worthless offerings; they are as a loathsome incense to me. As for convening meetings at the New Month and on the Sabbath, wickedness with the solemn gathering I cannot approve.

14 Your monthly and regular meetings my soul detests. They have become a burden on me; I am weary of putting up with them.

15 When you spread forth your hands, I will conceal my eyes from you; though you pray at length, I will not hear— your hands are filled with blood.

16 Wash yourselves clean: remove your wicked deeds from before my eyes; cease to do evil.

17 Learn to do good: demand justice, stand up for the oppressed; plead the cause of the fatherless, appeal on behalf of the widow. (Isaiah 1, Gileadi Translation)

1 Proclaim it aloud without restraint; raise your voice like a trumpet! Declare to my people their transgressions, to the house of Jacob its sins.

2 Yet they importune me daily, eager to learn my ways, like a nation practicing righteousness and not forsaking the precepts of its God. They inquire of me concerning correct ordinances, desiring to draw nearer to God:

3 Why, when we fast, do you not notice? We afflict our bodies and you remain indifferent! It is because on your fast day you pursue your own ends and constrain all who toil for you.

4 You fast amid strife and contention, striking out savagely with the fist. Your present fasts are not such as to make your voice heard on high.

5 Is this the manner of fasting I have required, just a time for men to torment themselves? Is it only for bowing one's head like a reed and making one's bed of sackcloth and ashes? Do you call that a fast, a day of Jehovah's good graces?

6 Is not this the fast I require: To release from wrongful bondage, to untie the harness of the yoke, to set the oppressed at liberty and abolish all forms of subjection? 7 Is it not to share your food with the hungry, to bring home the wretchedly poor, and when you see men underclad to clothe them, and not to neglect your own kin?

8 Then shall your light break through like the dawn and your healing speedily appear; your righteousness will go before you, and the glory of Jehovah will be your rearguard.

9 Then, should you call, Jehovah will respond; should you cry, he will say, I am here. Indeed, if you will banish servitude from among you, and the pointing finger and offensive speech,

10 if you will give of your own to the hungry and satisfy the needs of the oppressed,

then shall your light dawn amid darkness and your twilight become as the noonday.

11 Jehovah will direct you continually; he will satisfy your needs in the dearth and bring vigor to your limbs. And you will become like a well-watered garden, like a spring of unfailing waters.

12 They who came out of you will rebuild the ancient ruins; you will restore the foundations of generations ago. You shall be called a rebuilder of fallen walls, a restorer of streets for resettlement.

13 If you will keep your feet from trampling the Sabbath— from achieving your own ends on my holy day—and consider the Sabbath a delight, the holy day of Jehovah venerable, and if you will honor it by refraining from your everyday pursuits— from occupying yourselves with your own affairs and speaking of business matters—

14 then shall you delight in Jehovah, and I will make you traverse the heights of the earth and nourish you with the heritage of Jacob your father. By his mouth Jehovah has spoken it. (Isaiah 58, Gileadi Translation)

The strength of your connection with God will be a factor of how fully you keep God's commandments, how intently you worship God, how much desire you have to commune with him, how humble you are before him, how much you revere him, and your level of compassion for others.

What we should pray for comes from God through the Holy Ghost. "For behold, again I say unto you that if ye will enter in by the way, and receive the Holy Ghost, it will show unto you all things what ye should do." (2 Nephi 32:5) Each time you pray you must make this connection. Typically, this connection is established through worship. Other ways to establish it include remarkable intent, such as when you are unusually distraught, have a burning desire to commune with God, have a heart broken to pieces in compassion for another's suffering, or are in immediate danger.

The process of establishing a connection with God so that he can tell you what to pray for takes far more effort than asking things from God. Once you connect to God through the Holy Ghost, a powerful prayer will flow through you without much effort on your part, like water flowing downhill. This inspiration comes as we focus on God and what God wants. "In all thy ways acknowledge him, and he shall direct thy paths." (Proverbs 3:6)

Most prayers are ineffective because they reverse the process. They rush through or skip the process of establishing a connection with God, and jump right into the asking. These types of prayers are unlikely to be effective.

Once we successfully establish a connection and are asking according to God's will, we obtain answers to our prayers through several techniques that will always result in getting answers to every prayer—either in the form of a granted request or a reason why God will not grant it. Several chapters in this book are dedicated to some of these prayer strategies.

Understanding the routing mechanism for answered prayer can help you pray in a way that results in response. The government of God consists of far more than just God. Your prayers must not only be granted by God, but be considered by him in the first place. Though God knows all things, including the content of your prayers, the scriptures reveal a mechanism whereby our prayer requests are granted. Many prayers remain unanswered because we choose to ignore what the scriptures reveal about that mechanism, and replace it with the traditional naïve construct of treating prayers to God like a wishing well.

The routing mechanism is akin to how sacrifices were routed in the temple. The supplicant brought a sacrifice to door of the tabernacle. The lower priests received it, prepared it, and offered it on the altar in the outer portion of the tabernacle. They were the interface between the people and the high priest, and their office sanctified and added significance to the contribution of the supplicant. There was also a high priest. The high priest used the fire from the altar from the outer portion of the tabernacle to light the incense of the inner portion of the tabernacle, making another offering in holier spaces to combine with the offering from the supplicant burned on the altar. The supplicant's offering of animal flesh, despite sanctifying rules of purity concerning the animal, was consummately rooted in fleshy limitations. It was a bloody sacrifice, it was intertwined in source and use with carnal food, and its burning resulted in smoke that wasn't particularly pleasing to smell. The incense, on the other hand, was made fresh daily of rare and expensive ingredients. It was prepared according to an exacting recipe whose duplication for any other use was strictly prohibited. It was a more holy offering, with a strong, sweet odor.

Like rising smoke, the Holy Ghost takes your prayer to heaven. There, the heavenly priests collect the prayers of mankind:

> And when he had taken the book, the four beasts and four and twenty elders fell down before the Lamb, having every one of them harps, and golden vials full of odours, which are the prayers of saints. (Revelation 5:8)

Like the priests on earth, heavenly beings add independent, more holy offerings to your prayers:

> 2 And I saw the seven angels which stood before God; and to them were given seven trumpets.
> 3 And another angel came and stood at the altar, having a golden censer; and there was given unto him much incense, that he should offer it with the prayers of all saints upon the golden altar which was before the throne.
> 4 And the smoke of the incense, which came with the prayers of the saints, ascended up before God out of the angel's hand. (Revelation 8)

After collection, consideration, and addition by other heavenly beings, the Lord evaluates your request. The Lord is our high priest in heaven. If he supports it, he will take it to the Father, through whom all prayers are finally answered.

Now, none of us are aware of our prayers ascending to heaven. We do not see them routed through the heavenly authorities. We do not see the Lord interceding for us with the Father. So why do the mechanics matter?

The reason this process is critical to understand is so that we know the criteria for success and can engineer our prayers to be successful every time we offer them.

At any stage, the prayers can be rejected. How do your prayers get past heavenly beings (angels, elders, creatures, etc.)? What causes them to support your cause? What will inspire them to plead for you? They are constantly observing our lives, and taking a record of what they observe. In a sense, they are our first-line judges. Part of their mission is to minister to "...them of strong faith and a firm mind in every form of godliness." (Moroni 7:30) Prayers are forwarded by and added to by the angels according to our faith and our diligence in all of God's commands. In other words, our requests are amplified by heavenly beings inasmuch as we are true and faithful in all things. Angels can be our advocates with the Lord, or witnesses against us, depending on our righteousness.

In spite of the channel through the angels, there is also a channel directly to the Lord. The Lord Jesus is a singular king. While he presides over a vast heavenly government, he also reserves a personal, intimate involvement with each of us:

> O then, my beloved brethren, come unto the Lord, the Holy One. Remember that his paths are righteous. Behold, the way for man is narrow, but it lieth in a straight course before him, and the keeper of the gate is the Holy One of Israel; and he employeth no servant there; and there is none other way save it be by the gate; for he cannot be deceived, for the Lord God is his name. (2 Nephi 9:41)

In spite of our nothingness, through the unfathomable grace of God, our faith can be sufficient to provide direct, inalienable access to the Lord Jesus Christ.

The following story from the mortal ministry of the Savior represents both how we have direct access to God and how, through mighty faith in the Lord's goodness, we can bypass the heavenly authorities and gain direct access to the Lord:

> 35 And it came to pass, that as he was come nigh unto Jericho, a certain blind man sat by the way side begging:
> 36 And hearing the multitude pass by, he asked what it meant.
> 37 And they told him, that Jesus of Nazareth passeth by.
> 38 And he cried, saying, Jesus, thou Son of David, have mercy on me.
> 39 And they which went before rebuked him, that he should hold his peace: but he cried so much the more, Thou Son of David, have mercy on me.
> 40 And Jesus stood, and commanded him to be brought unto him: and when he was come near, he asked him,
> 41 Saying, What wilt thou that I shall do unto thee? And he said, Lord, that I may receive my sight.
> 42 And Jesus said unto him, Receive thy sight: thy faith hath saved thee.
> 43 And immediately he received his sight, and followed him, glorifying God: and all the people, when they saw it, gave praise unto God. (Luke 18)

Instead of transmitting the message to the Lord, those that went before the Lord tried to silence the cries of the blind man. This did not deter the blind man. He cried even louder and with even more earnest, until Jesus himself heard him and acknowledged him.

Another example of bypassing the heavenly hierarchy is given by Hezekiah. Isaiah, a prophet of God, delivered the word of the Lord that Hezekiah would die at a young age:

> 1 In those days was Hezekiah sick unto death. And Isaiah the prophet the son of Amoz came unto him, and said unto him, Thus saith the Lord, Set thine house in order: for thou shalt die, and not live.
> 2 Then Hezekiah turned his face toward the wall, and prayed unto the Lord,

3 And said, Remember now, O Lord, I beseech thee, how I have walked before thee in truth and with a perfect heart, and have done that which is good in thy sight. And Hezekiah wept sore.

4 Then came the word of the Lord to Isaiah, saying,

5 Go, and say to Hezekiah, Thus saith the Lord, the God of David thy father, I have heard thy prayer, I have seen thy tears: behold, I will add unto thy days fifteen years.

6 And I will deliver thee and this city out of the hand of the king of Assyria: and I will defend this city.

7 And this shall be a sign unto thee from the Lord, that the Lord will do this thing that he hath spoken;

8 Behold, I will bring again the shadow of the degrees, which is gone down in the sun dial of Ahaz, ten degrees backward. So the sun returned ten degrees, by which degrees it was gone down. (Isaiah 38)

In response to the Lord's word, Hezekiah pleaded with God *directly* to spare his life. God heard and answered his prayer. He sent word once again through Isaiah that his life would be extended.

What kinds of prayers are granted by the Lord? He is our advocate with the Father (see 1 John 2:1). What causes the Lord to intercede for your cause? The Lord loves all his children, but he bestows special favor on the righteous. "Behold, the Lord esteemeth all flesh in one; he that is righteous is favored of God…." (1 Nephi 17:35) The Lord Jesus supports those who believe in him. The Amplified Bible, a translation that attempts to recover the breadth of original meaning lost in translation from the source languages to English, describes *believe* as "adhere to, trust in, and rely on." This is a beautiful definition that transcends our normal understanding of the word. When we adhere to, trust in, and rely on the Lord, we will successfully obtain his attention. He will bring us near to him and ask us what we want. That is the connection we seek.

Those that adhere to, trust in, and rely on the Lord will frame their prayers in terms of the Lord's will. After all, if we are focused on our own will, we are adhering to, trusting in, and relying upon ourselves instead of him. We arouse the Lord's advocacy when we frame our communication with him in terms of his attributes and his promises. God has made many promises to men, and he is bound to them by his faithfulness. God's attributes are also a gateway to answered prayer. God is just (always consistent, always fulfills his promises), he is merciful (quick to forgive, slow to anger), he is loving (desires to bless, desires to fulfill desires of children), he supports the oppressed, he fulfills his promises, and he is a warrior. Leveraging the Lord's characteristics and promises will result in answered prayer. This process is discussed in later chapters.

When you ask, seek, and knock, you are not fawning to obtain the fickle favor of an arbitrary God. God is not arbitrary, and he is not fickle. God already wills to give you greater blessings than you can imagine: "But as it is written, Eye hath not seen, nor ear heard, neither have entered into the heart of man, the things which God hath prepared for them that love him." (1 Corinthians 2:9) The lack of desired blessings in your life is not a result of God's contrary will, but of your contrary heart. The effect of crying to the Lord is not changing God's mind, but changing your heart. As you cry, you submit.

Submission to God results in answered prayer because it results in requests according to the will of God, and the Lord grants requests that align with his will.

Some prayers go unfulfilled in spite of them being God's will because the supplicant is not yet ready to receive them. All blessings correspond to certain levels of commandments, and until a person has obeyed the corresponding commandments, it would be a curse to bestow the requested blessing. Often, requests for blessings are answered with a test from God so you can see for yourself whether or not you will obey him. We tend to think we are better than we are. Tests are a gift from God to help you discover your self-deception. God's tests show you what your desires truly are—how different your desires are than his, and how different they are than what you would like to think.

Sometimes that test is explicit, but most times it comes without being noticed. Sometimes, granting a prayer request requires the Lord to teach the supplicant new things, new things that they are not yet quite ready for. Our obedience and humility can be significant limiting factors in what requests God can grant.

As you submit to God, you prepare your heart to receive a new commandment or obey an old one. You actually increase your capacity for obedience. As you yield your heart to God, you become sanctified because your capacity for obedience increases:

> Nevertheless they did fast and pray oft, and did wax stronger and stronger in their humility, and firmer and

firmer in the faith of Christ, unto the filling their souls with joy and consolation, yea, even to the purifying and the sanctification of their hearts, which sanctification cometh because of their yielding their hearts unto God. (Helaman 3:35)

Once you have sufficiently increased in capacity, God can send you the blessings corresponding to the teachings you have obeyed, which might include new teachings he will reveal to you as part of the process.

On a final note, when we seek God for what to pray for, let us consider that God is so much greater than any material blessing. Any father delights when his children ask him to share his wisdom with them, rather than simply asking for material goods. The greatest blessing he can give us is a habitation with him—to focus on having him instead of having some subset of what he has. It brings him great joy when this is our chief desire and a subject of all our prayers.

Leveraging God's Promises in Prayer

...whatever I say will be fulfilled. (Ezekiel 12:28, NIV)

Throughout time, God has made promises to his people. God does not violate his promises. One sure way to move heaven is to prayerfully invoke the promises God has made through our faith in God's trustworthiness.

Jacob invoked God's promises when he prayed for God's protection in returning to his previously hostile brother after years away:

> 9 And Jacob said, O God of my father Abraham, and God of my father Isaac, the Lord which saidst unto me, Return unto thy country, and to thy kindred, and I will deal well with thee:
> 10 I am not worthy of the least of all the mercies, and of all the truth, which thou hast shewed unto thy servant; for with my staff I passed over this Jordan; and now I am become two bands.
> 11 Deliver me, I pray thee, from the hand of my brother, from the hand of Esau: for I fear him, lest he will come and smite me, and the mother with the children.
> 12 And thou saidst, I will surely do thee good, and make thy seed as the sand of the sea, which cannot be numbered for multitude. (Gen 32:9-12)

Jacob said, "God, you told me that if I came home, everything would be well with me. You told me that you would bless me and make my seed as the sand of the sea. That blessing cannot be fulfilled if I am destroyed by my brother. Please protect me." He invoked two of God's blessings, and as a result, Esau's wrath was miraculously abated.

Elijah invoked God's promises. In his famous encounter with the priests of Baal, he prayed and reminded God that he had told Elijah to hold this demonstration:

> 36 And it came to pass at the time of the offering of the evening sacrifice, that Elijah the prophet came near, and said, Lord God of Abraham, Isaac, and of Israel, let it be known this day that thou art God in Israel, and that I am thy servant, and that I have done all these things at thy word.
> 37 Hear me, O Lord, hear me, that this people may know that thou art the Lord God, and that thou hast turned their heart back again.
> 38 Then the fire of the Lord fell, and consumed the burnt sacrifice, and the wood, and the stones, and the dust, and licked up the water that was in the trench. (1 Kings 18)

In other words, he was saying "Lord, you've told me to do this, and now I have done it. Please do what you said you were going to do, and send fire to consume this sacrifice, that your promise may be fulfilled."

David received great promises from the Lord, and they brought him great peace despite a tumultuous life:

> 25 And now, O Lord God, the word that thou hast spoken concerning thy servant, and concerning his house, establish it for ever, and do as thou hast said.
> 26 And let thy name be magnified for ever, saying, The Lord of hosts is the God over Israel: and let the house of thy servant David be established before thee.
> 27 For thou, O Lord of hosts, God of Israel, hast revealed to thy servant, saying, I will build thee an house: therefore hath thy servant found in his heart to pray this prayer unto thee.
> 28 And now, O Lord God, thou art that God, and thy words be true, and thou hast promised this goodness unto thy servant:
> 29 Therefore now let it please thee to bless the house of thy servant, that it may continue for ever before thee: for thou, O Lord God, hast spoken it: and with thy blessing

let the house of thy servant be blessed for ever. (2 Samuel 7)

You can be bold with God when he has not fulfilled his promises. Consider Moses' attitude when he reminds God of his promise to deliver the people:

> 22 And Moses returned unto the Lord, and said, Lord, wherefore hast thou so evil entreated this people? why is it that thou hast sent me?
> 23 For since I came to Pharaoh to speak in thy name, he hath done evil to this people; neither hast thou delivered thy people at all. (Exodus 5:22-23)

We can see that having personal promises from God are one key to miraculous responses to prayer. Promises are invoked through prayer, but they are also largely obtained through prayer.

Whether God has given you promises or not, with great skill, you can leverage promises God has made to others. On one occasion when God wanted to destroy the Israelites, Moses interceded for them by reminding God of the promises he had made to Abraham, Isaac, and Israel:

> 9 And the Lord said unto Moses, I have seen this people, and, behold, it is a stiffnecked people:
> 10 Now therefore let me alone, that my wrath may wax hot against them, and that I may consume them: and I will make of thee a great nation.
> 11 And Moses besought the Lord his God, and said, Lord, why doth thy wrath wax hot against thy people...?
> 13 Remember Abraham, Isaac, and Israel, thy servants, to whom thou swarest by thine own self, and saidst unto them, I will multiply your seed as the stars of heaven, and all this land that I have spoken of will I give unto your seed, and they shall inherit it for ever.
> 14 And the Lord repented of the evil which he thought to do unto his people. (Exodus 32)

Though the blessings were to Abraham, Isaac, and Israel, their fulfillment required the survival of the Israelites.

God's promises do not expire. Nehemiah invoked promises made many years earlier through Moses:

> 7 We have dealt very corruptly against thee, and have not kept the commandments, nor the statutes, nor the judgments, which thou commandedst thy servant Moses.
> 8 Remember, I beseech thee, the word that thou commandedst thy servant Moses, saying, If ye transgress, I will scatter you abroad among the nations:
> 9 But if ye turn unto me, and keep my commandments, and do them; though there were of you cast out unto the uttermost part of the heaven, yet will I gather them from thence, and will bring them unto the place that I have chosen to set my name there.
> 10 Now these are thy servants and thy people, whom thou hast redeemed by thy great power, and by thy strong hand.
> 11 O Lord, I beseech thee, let now thine ear be attentive to the prayer of thy servant, and to the prayer of thy servants, who desire to fear thy name: and prosper, I pray thee, thy servant this day, and grant him mercy in the sight of this man. For I was the king's cupbearer. (Nehemiah 1)

Nehemiah's people were in captivity. He said, "Lord, you promised that if we repent and turn to you, you will gather us. We have repented, so please turn the heart of the king so that we can return to our land."

There are many promises God has made not to specific people, but to anyone who fulfills certain conditions. Your ability to leverage God's promises in prayer is limited to your knowledge of his promises. A sustained study of the scriptures to extract promises that could be useful in prayer will significantly increase your power in invoking his promises.

Consider the abundant promises you can invoke if you have kept all of God's commandments. If you are overwhelmed, you can remind the Lord of his promises: "Come unto me, all ye that labour and are heavy laden, and I will give you rest." (Matthew 11:28) "I will not leave you comfortless: I will come to you." (John 14:18)

If you need to witness to others, you can count on him to give you what to say:

> 11 And when they bring you unto the synagogues, and unto magistrates, and powers, take ye no thought how or what thing ye shall answer, or what ye shall say:
> 12 For the Holy Ghost shall teach you in the same hour what ye ought to say. (Luke 12)

You can remind God of his promise to provide for the righteous:

> Therefore take no thought, saying, what shall we eat? or, what shall we drink? or, wherewithal shall we be clothed? But seek ye first the kingdom of God, and his righteousness; and all these things shall be added unto you. (Matthew 6:31,33)

You can ask anything according to God's will and have it done. "If ye abide in me, and my words abide in you, ye shall ask what ye will, and it shall be done unto you." (John 15:7) "Verily, verily, I say unto you, Whatsoever ye shall ask the Father in my name, he will give it you." (John 16:3)

You can invoke the promise of obtaining the Spirit:

> But the Comforter, which is the Holy Ghost, whom the Father will send in my name, he shall teach you all things, and bring all things to your remembrance, whatsoever I have said unto you. (John 14:26)

> And we are his witnesses of these things; and so is also the Holy Ghost, whom God hath given to them that obey him. (Acts 5:32)

You can even invoke the promise of his presence:

> If any man serve me, let him follow me; and where I am, there shall also my servant be: if any man serve me, him will my Father honour. (John 12:26)

He that hath my commandments, and keepeth them, he it is that loveth me: and he that loveth me shall be loved of my Father, and I will love him, and will manifest myself to him. (John 14:21)

Jesus answered and said unto him, If a man love me, he will keep my words: and my Father will love him, and we will come unto him, and make our abode with him. (John 14:23)

Truly, as the Lord said, "blessed are they that hear the word of God, and keep it." (Luke 11:28)

Leveraging God's Character in Prayer

He loveth righteousness and judgment: the earth is full of the goodness of the Lord. (Psalm 33:5)

God's character is the same yesterday, today, and forever. Among other things, he is holy, all-knowing, merciful, loving, just, and trustworthy. Those who know and leverage these traits will be successful in obtaining answered prayers.

Do not mistake leveraging God's character as somehow forcing God's hand. There is no coercion or magic in this technique. Rather, it is the fulfillment of what God has asked us to do. It is the fulfillment of his commandment for us to ask, seek, and knock with faith in him.

Faith opens the door to miracles that wouldn't otherwise happen. Faith is much more than belief, it is belief in something that is true. By identifying situations where God's character suggests his intervention, you can exercise your faith in him to bring about miracles that wouldn't otherwise happen.

To illustrate the connection between faith and leveraging God's attributes, consider the story of the Canaanite woman who successfully obtained a miracle from the Lord.

> 22 And, behold, a woman of Canaan came out of the same coasts, and cried unto him, saying, Have mercy on me, O Lord, thou Son of David; my daughter is grievously vexed with a devil.
>
> 23 But he answered her not a word. And his disciples came and besought him, saying, Send her away; for she crieth after us.
>
> 24 But he answered and said, I am not sent but unto the lost sheep of the house of Israel.

25 Then came she and worshipped him, saying, Lord, help me.

26 But he answered and said, It is not meet to take the children's bread, and to cast it to dogs.

27 And she said, Truth, Lord: yet the dogs eat of the crumbs which fall from their masters' table.

28 Then Jesus answered and said unto her, O woman, great is thy faith: be it unto thee even as thou wilt. And her daughter was made whole from that very hour. (Matthew 15)

The woman knew that the Lord was merciful. She invoked his mercy. Even when he told her all the reasons he could not do as she asked, she pressed on. She knew that the Lord's mercy was greater than all of those reasons. She was right. In granting her request, he commended her by saying, "O woman, great is thy faith."

The Lord wants to bless us with far more blessings than we actually receive. Our failure to invoke his character in our petitions is one reason for this.

One of God's characteristics is mercy. As demonstrated by his answer to the Canaanite woman, the Lord is merciful to those who lean upon him in total submission. Another example of this is found in Matthew 20:

30 And, behold, two blind men sitting by the way side, when they heard that Jesus passed by, cried out, saying, Have mercy on us, O Lord, thou Son of David.

31 And the multitude rebuked them, because they should hold their peace: but they cried the more, saying, Have mercy on us, O Lord, thou Son of David.

32 And Jesus stood still, and called them, and said, What will ye that I shall do unto you?

33 They say unto him, Lord, that our eyes may be opened.

The disciples tried to quiet these men. Instead of being daunted, they cried even louder! Imagine these men—imagine their intensity in crying. They truly had full trust in the Lord. The angels are not as merciful as the Lord is. Cry right past them! Contrition moves the Lord. He healed the ten lepers who said "Master, have mercy on us." (Luke 17:13) He forgave the sins of the contrite publican:

> 10 Two men went up into the temple to pray; the one a Pharisee, and the other a publican.
>
> 11 The Pharisee stood and prayed thus with himself, God, I thank thee, that I am not as other men are, extortioners, unjust, adulterers, or even as this publican.
>
> 12 I fast twice in the week, I give tithes of all that I possess.
>
> 13 And the publican, standing afar off, would not lift up so much as his eyes unto heaven, but smote upon his breast, saying, God be merciful to me a sinner.
>
> 14 I tell you, this man went down to his house justified rather than the other: for every one that exalteth himself shall be abased; and he that humbleth himself shall be exalted. (Luke 18)

The Lord is merciful to those who lean on him.

Abraham knew God's character. He knew that God would not destroy the wicked with the righteous. He invoked God's justice in an attempt to spare Sodom and Gomorrah from destruction:

> 22 And the men turned their faces from thence, and went toward Sodom: but Abraham stood yet before the Lord.
>
> 23 And Abraham drew near, and said, Wilt thou also destroy the righteous with the wicked?
>
> 24 Peradventure there be fifty righteous within the city: wilt thou also destroy and not spare the place for the fifty righteous that are therein?
>
> 25 That be far from thee to do after this manner, to slay the righteous with the wicked: and that the righteous should be as the wicked, that be far from thee: Shall not the Judge of all the earth do right?
>
> 26 And the Lord said, If I find in Sodom fifty righteous within the city, then I will spare all the place for their sakes.

27 And Abraham answered and said, Behold now, I have taken upon me to speak unto the Lord, which am but dust and ashes:
28 Peradventure there shall lack five of the fifty righteous: wilt thou destroy all the city for lack of five? And he said, If I find there forty and five, I will not destroy it.
29 And he spake unto him yet again, and said, Peradventure there shall be forty found there. And he said, I will not do it for forty's sake.
30 And he said unto him, Oh let not the Lord be angry, and I will speak: Peradventure there shall thirty be found there. And he said, I will not do it, if I find thirty there.
31 And he said, Behold now, I have taken upon me to speak unto the Lord: Peradventure there shall be twenty found there. And he said, I will not destroy it for twenty's sake.
32 And he said, Oh let not the Lord be angry, and I will speak yet but this once: Peradventure ten shall be found there. And he said, I will not destroy it for ten's sake. (Genesis 18:22-32)

God loves us and does mighty works to help us have faith. He realizes that men will struggle to have faith in a God who appears to be inconsistent, fickle, or weak. We can leverage his desire to help men see his greatness.

Elijah invoked the justice of God in behalf of the widow whose son died. This woman had sacrificed much for the benefit of Elijah because he was a man of God. Elijah reminded the Lord of the woman's kindness to him, as well as the inevitable ill effect of the death of the son on his ministry and God's reputation:

20 And he cried unto the Lord, and said, O Lord my God, hast thou also brought evil upon the widow with whom I sojourn, by slaying her son?
21 And he stretched himself upon the child three times, and cried unto the Lord, and said, O Lord my God, I pray thee, let this child's soul come into him again.

22 And the Lord heard the voice of Elijah; and the soul of the child came into him again, and he revived. (1 Kings 17)

Moses frequently leveraged God's reputation to intercede for Israel. He reminded God that if he destroyed the Israelites:

13 …the Egyptians shall hear it, (for thou broughtest up this people in thy might from among them;)
14 And they will tell it to the inhabitants of this land: for they have heard that thou Lord art among this people, that thou Lord art seen face to face, and that thy cloud standeth over them, and that thou goest before them, by day time in a pillar of a cloud, and in a pillar of fire by night.
15 Now if thou shalt kill all this people as one man, then the nations which have heard the fame of thee will speak, saying,
16 Because the Lord was not able to bring this people into the land which he sware unto them, therefore he hath slain them in the wilderness.
17 And now, I beseech thee, let the power of my Lord be great, according as thou hast spoken, saying,
18 The Lord is longsuffering, and of great mercy, forgiving iniquity and transgression, and by no means clearing the guilty, visiting the iniquity of the fathers upon the children unto the third and fourth generation.
19 Pardon, I beseech thee, the iniquity of this people according unto the greatness of thy mercy, and as thou hast forgiven this people, from Egypt even until now. (Numbers 14)

He focused on the fact that the surrounding nations would interpret their destruction as his inability to deliver them:

26 I prayed therefore unto the Lord, and said, O Lord God, destroy not thy people and thine inheritance, which thou hast redeemed through thy greatness, which thou hast brought forth out of Egypt with a mighty hand.

28 Lest the land whence thou broughtest us out say, Because the Lord was not able to bring them into the land which he promised them, and because he hated them, he hath brought them out to slay them in the wilderness. (Deuteronomy 9)

9 And the Lord said unto Moses, I have seen this people, and, behold, it is a stiffnecked people:
10 Now therefore let me alone, that my wrath may wax hot against them, and that I may consume them: and I will make of thee a great nation.
11 And Moses besought the Lord his God, and said, Lord, why doth thy wrath wax hot against thy people, which thou hast brought forth out of the land of Egypt with great power, and with a mighty hand?
12 Wherefore should the Egyptians speak, and say, For mischief did he bring them out, to slay them in the mountains, and to consume them from the face of the earth? Turn from thy fierce wrath, and repent of this evil against thy people.
13 Remember Abraham, Isaac, and Israel, thy servants, to whom thou swarest by thine own self, and saidst unto them, I will multiply your seed as the stars of heaven, and all this land that I have spoken of will I give unto your seed, and they shall inherit it for ever.
14 And the Lord repented of the evil which he thought to do unto his people. (Exodus 32)

Without Moses' skillful leveraging of God's attributes in behalf of Israel, they would have been destroyed. Though this prayer strategy is simple, it can be used to work great miracles.

When the Assyrians threatened Israel, Hezekiah sought the Lord's protection through invoking his jealousy. He brought to the Lord the Assyrian general's mockery of the Lord:

15 And Hezekiah prayed before the Lord, and said, O Lord God of Israel, which dwellest between the cherubims, thou art the God, even thou alone, of all the kingdoms of the earth; thou hast made heaven and earth.

16 Lord, bow down thine ear, and hear: open, Lord, thine eyes, and see: and hear the words of Sennacherib, which hath sent him to reproach the living God.

17 Of a truth, Lord, the kings of Assyria have destroyed the nations and their lands,

18 And have cast their gods into the fire: for they were no gods, but the work of men's hands, wood and stone: therefore they have destroyed them.

19 Now therefore, O Lord our God, I beseech thee, save thou us out of his hand, that all the kingdoms of the earth may know that thou art the Lord God, even thou only. (2 Kings 19)

Hezekiah pointed out how God's action against the Assyrians would distinguish God from the false gods of previously defeated kingdoms. By crushing the Assyrians, God could help men have faith in him. The Lord destroyed the Assyrians in a day in a great miracle. Hezekiah's tack was very wise, as his righteousness was not mirrored by his people, and it would have been difficult to make a case for intervention from God by pleading for his people directly.

Nothing is impossible with God, and he enjoys proving this to men. Consider the Lord's reaction when his servants were unable to help one particular child:

15 Lord, have mercy on my son: for he is lunatic, and sore vexed: for ofttimes he falleth into the fire, and oft into the water.

16 And I brought him to thy disciples, and *they could not cure him.*

17 Then Jesus answered and said, O faithless and perverse generation, how long shall I be with you? how long shall I suffer you? bring him hither to me.

18 And Jesus rebuked the devil; and he departed out of him: and the child was cured from that very hour. (Matthew 17)

We can leverage his omnipotence by providing opportunities for him to do what is impossible with men.

The Lord is merciful. We can invoke God's mercy, as Nehemiah did:

189

And said, I beseech thee, O Lord God of heaven, the great and terrible God, that keepeth covenant and mercy for them that love him and observe his commandments: (Nehemiah 1:5)

The Lord is just. Those who know this can invoke his justice:

And they cried with a loud voice, saying, How long, O Lord, holy and true, dost thou not judge and avenge our blood on them that dwell on the earth? (Revelation 6:10)

The Lord delights to bless those who love him. Righteous king Hezekiah was able to secure a blessing from God by asking him to "remember now how I have walked before thee in truth and with a perfect heart, and have done that which is good in thy sight...." (2 Kings 20:3) Moses frequently employed this tactic. On one occasion he said:

12 And Moses said unto the Lord, See, thou sayest unto me, Bring up this people: and thou hast not let me know whom thou wilt send with me. Yet thou hast said, I know thee by name, and thou hast also found grace in my sight.
13 Now therefore, I pray thee, if I have found grace in thy sight, shew me now thy way, that I may know thee, that I may find grace in thy sight: and consider that this nation is thy people.
14 And he said, My presence shall go with thee, and I will give thee rest.
15 And he said unto him, If thy presence go not with me, carry us not up hence.
16 For wherein shall it be known here that I and thy people have found grace in thy sight? is it not in that thou goest with us? so shall we be separated, I and thy people, from all the people that are upon the face of the earth.
17 And the Lord said unto Moses, I will do this thing also that thou hast spoken: for thou hast found grace in my sight, and I know thee by name. (Exodus 33)

King David asked the Lord to bless his son Solomon and the people in recognition of his acquiring materials for a temple in the "uprightness of [his] heart":

> 16 O Lord our God, all this store that we have prepared to build thee an house for thine holy name cometh of thine hand, and is all thine own.
>
> 17 I know also, my God, that thou triest the heart, and hast pleasure in uprightness. As for me, in the uprightness of mine heart I have willingly offered all these things: and now have I seen with joy thy people, which are present here, to offer willingly unto thee.
>
> 18 O Lord God of Abraham, Isaac, and of Israel, our fathers, keep this for ever in the imagination of the thoughts of the heart of thy people, and prepare their heart unto thee:
>
> 19 And give unto Solomon my son a perfect heart, to keep thy commandments, thy testimonies, and thy statutes, and to do all these things, and to build the palace, for the which I have made provision. (1 Chronicles 29)

The Lord is the definition of selflessness. He recognizes this trait in his servants. Seeking blessings on behalf of others is one way to move heaven. Solomon's prayer for wisdom was answered because he asked for it not for his own benefit, but for the benefit of his people:

> 6 And Solomon said, Thou hast shewed unto thy servant David my father great mercy, according as he walked before thee in truth, and in righteousness, and in uprightness of heart with thee; and thou hast kept for him this great kindness, that thou hast given him a son to sit on his throne, as it is this day.
>
> 7 And now, O Lord my God, thou hast made thy servant king instead of David my father: and I am but a little child: I know not how to go out or come in.
>
> 8 And thy servant is in the midst of thy people which thou hast chosen, a great people, that cannot be numbered nor counted for multitude.

9 Give therefore thy servant an understanding heart to judge thy people, that I may discern between good and bad: for who is able to judge this thy so great a people? 10 And the speech pleased the Lord, that Solomon had asked this thing. (1 Kings 3)

More about how to seek blessings for others is explained in the next chapter.

The Lord is willing to work mighty miracles for those who invoke his righteousness in faith. Learning God's attributes and leveraging them in prayer is one way to secure answers to our prayers.

Intercession

Love never fails. But where there are prophecies, they will cease; where there are tongues, they will be stilled; where there is knowledge, it will pass away. (1 Corinthians 13:8, NIV)

God is exceptionally merciful, more than we can imagine. Yet, he is also just. The dynamic between these two qualities is something that, when understood, can be navigated to yield a stronger, more fruitful connection with God.

God loves us so much that he wishes to give us many more blessings than we receive. What keeps us from receiving them? We do not possess the character or live the life associated with them. It is very common for God to want to bless an individual, but he is often curtailed in his ability to do so by his justice.

It is wrong to think that the Lord's sacrifice fulfilled all the demands of justice, making it possible to automatically receive anything we ask for. Through his sacrifice, the Lord Jesus made it possible for divine justice to endure while still extending forgiveness to those whose disobedience would otherwise subject them to punishment. He did not rob justice through his sacrifice, but rather satisfied it with his sacrifice. He paid the price of our penalty. Likewise, there is a price to pay for each blessing we seek.

Intercession gives us the ability to obtain otherwise unmerited blessings for others through our own sacrifice. Just as the Lord Jesus paid the price of our sin, making it possible for us to obtain forgiveness that we didn't earn, we can intercede for others to call down blessings on their behalf that they do not merit on their own. Even though the sacrifice on our part is miniscule compared to the sacrifice of Christ, the intervention of a righteous man can and does move heaven. "The effectual fervent prayer of a righteous man availeth much…" (James 5:16)

Intercession is a special kind of prayer for other people. Normal prayer for others—supplication—consists of asking the Lord to take care of something for someone else. In intercession, the praying person invests their heart and soul into the problem for the other person. Intercessors are willing to stand in the gap, or risk their own life and salvation for the person. They truly love those they pray for more than they love themselves. They pray as if their fate were tied up in the fate of those they pray for. In fact, they love those they pray for *more* than themselves, because they are willing to sacrifice their own wellbeing for those they pray for.

This kind of sacrifice tips the scales of justice by adding merit to the cause of the subject of prayer. By tipping the scales of justice, intercession can secure blessings that would otherwise not be secured: It postpones prescribed judgment, reduces prescribed judgment, extends new truth to men who could otherwise not obtain it, provides answers to prayers beyond what people would normally be willing or able to receive, and secures miracles.

Why would anyone want to pray like this, almost always for those who abuse you, and many times for those you don't even know well? "Greater love hath no man than this, that a man lay down his life for his friends." (John 15:13) You will be hard pressed to find a greater expression of charity than intercession. In fact, you can't have charity without intercession for others, and you can't conduct intercession for others if you don't have charity.

The Lord Jesus Christ is the great intercessor. We cannot follow his example without interceding for others. He sits at "the right hand of God, [and] maketh intercession for us." (Romans 8:34) Paul said "he ever liveth to make intercession for [us]." (Hebrews 7:25) Examples of his intercession include his atoning sacrifice, his condescension in coming to earth, how he forgives sins, and how he constantly pleads for us to the Father.

> My little children, these things write I unto you, that ye sin not. And if any man sin, we have an advocate with the Father, Jesus Christ the righteous: (1 John 2:1)

Without the Lord's intercession, the justice of God would require all of us to be immediately slain in our wickedness. The Lord advocates for each of us with the Father. Kneeling before him, he displays the marks in his hands and shows him his blood which was shed. He pleads, "Because of my righteous sacrifice, have mercy on them."

Just as he intercedes for you at the throne of the Father, you are to intercede for others at his throne. You become their advocate with the Lord as the Lord is our advocate with the Father. The Lord's joy is great when we emulate him. He is very close during intercession. He smiles upon those who do it. When you intercede for another, you are filled with the love that God feels for them. This draws you nearer to him.

The Lord Jesus is not the only intercessor. Intercession happens throughout his kingdom. A good example of the intercession that occurs at the throne of the Lord Jesus is given by the cherubim who stand beside it. Their form and function is described in the ark of the covenant:

> And the cherubims shall stretch forth their wings on high, covering the mercy seat with their wings, and their faces shall look one to another; toward the mercy seat shall the faces of the cherubims be. (Exodus 25:20)

These angels face the Lord, and form a two-way veil with their wings. From us, they veil the glory of the Lord, which would consume our flesh. From the Lord, they filter the wickedness of men. The name "mercy seat" comes from the fact that their mission is to constantly remind the Lord of his merciful nature. Their loud, constant cries of "Mercy! Mercy! Have mercy, Lord!" cover the violent noise produced by our sins.

As we intercede for others, we embark on the spiritual errands normally reserved for angels, who are constantly interceding with the Lord on behalf of men, preventing the outpouring of judgments that would otherwise justly occur.

Intercession is fully for the benefit of others, but you cannot intercede without receiving blessings yourself. Intercession brings you closer to God because it unlocks real intent in your heart that can propel and elevate your desire for righteousness and strengthen your connection to God. It will cause you to grow in compassion. Compassion is a quality that, unlike gifts of the Spirit, will persist in your character far after this life has ended.

1 Though I speak with the tongues of men and of angels, and have not charity, I am become as sounding brass, or a tinkling cymbal.

2 And though I have the gift of prophecy, and understand all mysteries, and all knowledge; and though I have all faith, so that I could remove mountains, and have not charity, I am nothing.

3 And though I bestow all my goods to feed the poor, and though I give my body to be burned, and have not charity, it profiteth me nothing.

4 Charity suffereth long, and is kind; charity envieth not; charity vaunteth not itself, is not puffed up,

5 Doth not behave itself unseemly, seeketh not her own, is not easily provoked, thinketh no evil;

6 Rejoiceth not in iniquity, but rejoiceth in the truth;

7 Beareth all things, believeth all things, hopeth all things, endureth all things.

8 Charity never faileth: but whether there be prophecies, they shall fail; whether there be tongues, they shall cease; whether there be knowledge, it shall vanish away.

9 For we know in part, and we prophesy in part.

10 But when that which is perfect is come, then that which is in part shall be done away.

11 When I was a child, I spake as a child, I understood as a child, I thought as a child: but when I became a man, I put away childish things.

12 For now we see through a glass, darkly; but then face to face: now I know in part; but then shall I know even as also I am known.

13 And now abideth faith, hope, charity, these three; but the greatest of these is charity. (1 Corinthians 13)

Compassionate prayer has a special power to pierce the heavens. When you have compassion for the subject of your prayer, your prayer will somehow overflow with fervor beyond what is found in your normal prayers.

In a strange way, compassion makes you willing to sacrifice your own needs for the needs of others, even when your needs are not trivial, and even when the benefit to the other person is less than the cost to you. This is an incredibly godly exercise, as it follows the Lord's example.

Intercession is crucial to the Lord having a people on earth. When God makes covenants with people, there are consequent curses that go along with the blessings should the people turn away. When they fall short, it is up to intercessors to stay the Lord's judgment and prolong their lives. To Ezekiel the Lord lamented: "I sought for a man among them, that should make up the hedge, and stand in the gap before me for the land, that I should not destroy it: but I found none." (Ezekiel 22:30)

It is possible for a people to be so wicked that even intercession cannot stay the Lord's judgment. In Ezekiel's time the people had become so wicked that the Lord said that even if Noah, Daniel, and Job were praying for Israel, they would be unable to deliver anyone but themselves (see Ezekiel 14:14). Eventually, a people can be so wicked that God says to stop praying for them:

> 7 O Lord, though our iniquities testify against us, do thou it for thy name's sake: for our backslidings are many; we have sinned against thee.
> 8 O the hope of Israel, the saviour thereof in time of trouble, why shouldest thou be as a stranger in the land, and as a wayfaring man that turneth aside to tarry for a night?
> 9 Why shouldest thou be as a man astonied, as a mighty man that cannot save? yet thou, O Lord, art in the midst of us, and we are called by thy name; leave us not.
> 10 Thus saith the Lord unto this people, Thus have they loved to wander, they have not refrained their feet, therefore the Lord doth not accept them; he will now remember their iniquity, and visit their sins.
> 11 Then said the Lord unto me, Pray not for this people for their good.
> 12 When they fast, I will not hear their cry; and when they offer burnt offering and an oblation, I will not accept them: but I will consume them by the sword, and by the famine, and by the pestilence. (Jeremiah 14)

Until then, we are under the admonition to "love your enemies, bless them that curse you, do good to them that hate you, and pray for them which despitefully use you, and persecute you." (Matthew 5:44)

Intercession requires sincere, patient, and intense sacrificial prayer. You may find yourself praying for someone for an entire day:

> 10 Now it came to pass that when Nephi, the son of Nephi, saw this wickedness of his people, his heart was exceedingly sorrowful.
> 11 And it came to pass that he went out and bowed himself down upon the earth, and cried mightily to his God in behalf of his people, yea, those who were about to be destroyed because of their faith in the tradition of their fathers.
> 12 And it came to pass that he cried mightily unto the Lord *all that day*; and behold, the voice of the Lord came unto him, saying: (3 Nephi 1)

You may find yourself fasting for three days or risking your life:

> 16 Go, gather together all the Jews that are present in Shushan, and fast ye for me, and neither eat nor drink three days, night or day: I also and my maidens will fast likewise; and so will I go in unto the king, which is not according to the law: and if I perish, I perish. (Esther 4)

You may find yourself fasting for forty days and forty nights:

> 18 And I fell down before the Lord, as at the first, forty days and forty nights: I did neither eat bread, nor drink water, because of all your sins which ye sinned, in doing wickedly in the sight of the Lord, to provoke him to anger.
> 19 For I was afraid of the anger and hot displeasure, wherewith the Lord was wroth against you to destroy you. But the Lord hearkened unto me at that time also. (Deuteronomy 9)

Self-abnegation for others produces results with God.

Like our prayers themselves, sacrifices have a critical mass commensurate with what we are asking for. Intercession in any significant way requires the person to present a significant sacrifice.

Typically, the person offers up their salvation or their life. The more righteous you are, the more weighty the sacrifice.

Moses once offered his salvation to God in order to spare the Israelites from destruction for worshiping the golden calf:

> 31 And Moses returned unto the Lord, and said, Oh, this people have sinned a great sin, and have made them gods of gold.
>
> 32 Yet now, if thou wilt forgive their sin—; and if not, blot me, I pray thee, out of thy book which thou hast written. (Exodus 32)

If Moses' name was not in the book of life, he could not have offered his salvation as a sacrifice for the sins of the people.

Those whose lives have not been spent in the service of God have less to offer, and those who have not yet obtained salvation cannot offer it in sacrifice.

Offers of sacrifice to God are serious. Do not make this offer to God unless you mean it. God sees all hearts, and he doesn't respond well to those who mock him. Moses was completely serious when he offered his salvation. On another occasion, he offered his life. In his case, God granted the requested action without requiring the sacrifice, but that doesn't mean he won't require it of others. John the Beloved provides another example of intercession. When he asked the Lord to delay his entrance into heaven so that he could bring more souls to the Lord, he was exercising intercession. The people did not deserve Moses, and they do not deserve John, but the sacrifices of Moses and John allowed a just God to transmit great blessings to them anyway.

Sacrifice isn't the only mechanism in intercession. All the prayer tactics discussed in this book apply, such as leveraging God's character and God's promises. For example, as Moses was receiving the ten commandments, God sent Moses down to the people to interrupt their worshipping of the golden calf. God told Moses he would destroy them. As he related later,

> 25 Thus I fell down before the Lord forty days and forty nights, as I fell down at the first; because the Lord had said he would destroy you.
>
> 26 I prayed therefore unto the Lord, and said, O Lord God, destroy not thy people and thine inheritance,

which thou hast redeemed through thy greatness, which thou hast brought forth out of Egypt with a mighty hand.

27 Remember thy servants, Abraham, Isaac, and Jacob; look not unto the stubbornness of this people, nor to their wickedness, nor to their sin:

28 Lest the land whence thou broughtest us out say, Because the Lord was not able to bring them into the land which he promised them, and because he hated them, he hath brought them out to slay them in the wilderness.

29 Yet they are thy people and thine inheritance, which thou broughtest out by thy mighty power and by thy stretched out arm. (Deuteronomy 9)

Most of the examples in the chapters on leveraging God's character and God's promises in prayer are examples of intercessory prayer. They are valid techniques, and they work.

Here is an example of Daniel applying the techniques in intercession. Notice how, despite the fact that he is righteous, he includes himself with those whose sins he is praying for. He is pleading for forgiveness of sins on behalf of people who have not yet repented. He also invokes the promise of God:

2 In the first year of his reign I Daniel understood by books the number of the years, whereof the word of the Lord came to Jeremiah the prophet, that he would accomplish seventy years in the desolations of Jerusalem.

3 And I set my face unto the Lord God, to seek by prayer and supplications, with fasting, and sackcloth, and ashes:

4 And I prayed unto the Lord my God, and made my confession, and said, O Lord, the great and dreadful God, keeping the covenant and mercy to them that love him, and to them that keep his commandments;

5 We have sinned, and have committed iniquity, and have done wickedly, and have rebelled, even by departing from thy precepts and from thy judgments:

6 Neither have we hearkened unto thy servants the prophets, which spake in thy name to our kings, our princes, and our fathers, and to all the people of the land.

7 O Lord, righteousness belongeth unto thee, but unto us confusion of faces, as at this day; to the men of Judah, and to the inhabitants of Jerusalem, and unto all Israel, that are near, and that are far off, through all the countries whither thou hast driven them, because of their trespass that they have trespassed against thee.

8 O Lord, to us belongeth confusion of face, to our kings, to our princes, and to our fathers, because we have sinned against thee.

9 To the Lord our God belong mercies and forgivenesses, though we have rebelled against him;

10 Neither have we obeyed the voice of the Lord our God, to walk in his laws, which he set before us by his servants the prophets.

11 Yea, all Israel have transgressed thy law, even by departing, that they might not obey thy voice; therefore the curse is poured upon us, and the oath that is written in the law of Moses the servant of God, because we have sinned against him.

12 And he hath confirmed his words, which he spake against us, and against our judges that judged us, by bringing upon us a great evil: for under the whole heaven hath not been done as hath been done upon Jerusalem.

13 As it is written in the law of Moses, all this evil is come upon us: yet made we not our prayer before the Lord our God, that we might turn from our iniquities, and understand thy truth.

14 Therefore hath the Lord watched upon the evil, and brought it upon us: for the Lord our God is righteous in all his works which he doeth: for we obeyed not his voice.

15 And now, O Lord our God, that hast brought thy people forth out of the land of Egypt with a mighty hand, and hast gotten thee renown, as at this day; we have sinned, we have done wickedly.

16 O Lord, according to all thy righteousness, I beseech thee, let thine anger and thy fury be turned away from

thy city Jerusalem, thy holy mountain: because for our sins, and for the iniquities of our fathers, Jerusalem and thy people are become a reproach to all that are about us.

17 Now therefore, O our God, hear the prayer of thy servant, and his supplications, and cause thy face to shine upon thy sanctuary that is desolate, for the Lord's sake.

18 O my God, incline thine ear, and hear; open thine eyes, and behold our desolations, and the city which is called by thy name: for we do not present our supplications before thee for our righteousnesses, but for thy great mercies.

19 O Lord, hear; O Lord, forgive; O Lord, hearken and do; defer not, for thine own sake, O my God: for thy city and thy people are called by thy name. (Daniel 9)

When you attempt to intercede for someone, be ready to have a conversation (even a debate) with God. He once said, "Come now, and let us reason together, saith the Lord..." (Isaiah 1:18) He wasn't speaking figuratively.

Elijah's experience with the widow's son gives us an example of how we can make a case with God in intercession:

16 And the barrel of meal wasted not, neither did the cruse of oil fail, according to the word of the Lord, which he spake by Elijah.

17 And it came to pass after these things, that the son of the woman, the mistress of the house, fell sick; and his sickness was so sore, that there was no breath left in him.

18 And she said unto Elijah, What have I to do with thee, O thou man of God? art thou come unto me to call my sin to remembrance, and to slay my son?

19 And he said unto her, Give me thy son. And he took him out of her bosom, and carried him up into a loft, where he abode, and laid him upon his own bed.

20 And he cried unto the Lord, and said, O Lord my God, hast thou also brought evil upon the widow with whom I sojourn, by slaying her son?

21 And he stretched himself upon the child three times, and cried unto the Lord, and said, O Lord my God, I pray thee, let this child's soul come into him again.

22 And the Lord heard the voice of Elijah; and the soul of the child came into him again, and he revived. (1 Kings 17)

Elijah's host had sacrificed a great deal to care for him. To have such tragedy befall her would irreparably damage her faith. Meanwhile, he was a well-known servant of God. If this sort of thing happened to those who helped him, what would that make people think about God? Elijah took this petition to God, and God granted for him to raise her son from the dead.

Much of the gospel is about rising to God's blessing through your consistent obedience, then condescending to sacrifice those blessings by sharing them with those who will not appreciate it or accept it. When you exercise mercy, especially in behalf of those you don't know, and especially in behalf of those who don't deserve it, you activate a law in heaven whereby God must act. God is much more merciful than any man, but he chooses to exercise mercy according to certain laws. For example, we are told that with what judgment we judge, we will be judged. There is no way to work around this law in this sphere of existence. Likewise, if we are righteous, we can place ourselves on the altar for the benefit of another and move heaven with our compassion to provide blessings to that person that they do not otherwise qualify for.

We should not underestimate the impact of intercession. Have you ever considered how it is possible that cities and nations far more wicked than Sodom and Gomorrah are not destroyed? It is because of many intercessions by the righteous on earth and in heaven. That is the scope and magnitude of the work of intercession. If it weren't for the intercession of the righteous, this world would have been destroyed a long time ago. Even on a much smaller scale, unseen intercessions by others impact your life every day.

God's kingdom runs on intercession. It's a hidden ministry of men, angels, and even the Lord. By learning this art and practicing it, you will have a significant impact on the Lord's work here on earth.

Opposition in All Things

Be sober, be vigilant; because your adversary the devil, as
a roaring lion, walketh about, seeking whom he may
devour: (1 Peter 5:8)

It is important to understand how Satan and his minions respond to your attempts to walk with God. There is opposition in all things:

> For it must needs be, that there is an opposition in all things. If not so, my firstborn in the wilderness, righteousness could not be brought to pass, neither wickedness, neither holiness nor misery, neither good nor bad. (2 Nephi 2:11)

When you attract the attention of heaven, you also attract the attention of hell. Hell's response is often not only more obvious to you than heaven's, but also can seem to happen faster and to a greater extent. The reason for this is that the devil's primary operating area is the body, where your perception is well-developed, while God's primary operating area is the spirit, where your perception is under-developed.

If your eyes were open to the spiritual realm, you would see how extensive, immediate, and mighty heaven's reaction can be to even your faintest attempts toward God.

> 8 Either what woman having ten pieces of silver, if she lose one piece, doth not light a candle, and sweep the house, and seek diligently till she find it?
> 9 And when she hath found it, she calleth her friends and her neighbours together, saying, Rejoice with me; for I have found the piece which I had lost.

10 Likewise, I say unto you, there is joy in the presence of the angels of God over one sinner that repenteth. (Luke 15)

There are several ways the devil reacts to your attempts to come to God, and understanding the devil's tactics gives you power over him. First, he counterfeits the interactions with God that you seek. Any form of interaction with God can be counterfeited by Satan: thoughts/impressions, dreams, voices, open visions, visitations, and so on. How frequently does this happen? Because there is opposition in all things, anyone who has had interactions with God has also had interactions with Satan. If you have had experiences with God, and don't know of any experiences you've had with Satan, you should prayerfully re-analyze your situation, because it is very likely that at least some of the experiences you think came from God were actually from Satan.

The easiest way to derail a seeker of truth is to provide them with some spiritual manifestation that surpasses their previous experience. The devil, having obtained great power and knowledge in the presence of God before his fall, can counterfeit almost anything that God can produce. He can give you impressions. He can speak to you. He can appear to you as an angel of light, and can even appear to you claiming to be God. He can work miracles.

The best time for Satan to try to pawn false experiences on you is when you are new to a certain class of experiences. When you feel impressions from the Holy Ghost for the first time, that or the next time is the most likely time he will send you a fake impression. When you hear the Lord's voice for the first time, that or the next time is the most likely time he will give you a voice-based revelation. He does this because you are unfamiliar with how revelations from God operate in that channel, and he is most likely to deceive you.

The second best time to deceive you is when you are particularly desperate for a connection with God, such as if you have sinned and are seeking repentance, or if it has been a while since you've heard from God.

Without great discernment, new and experienced believers alike have been led astray by spiritual counterfeits. Once Satan has enticed you with a demonic spiritual encounter, he can teach you false doctrine that will keep you busy with what you think will bring you to God, when it is actually keeping you from him. A great example of this is found in the story of Cain and Abel, where Cain was enticed by Satan to make an offering to God in a form other than what God had commanded.

How can you tell the difference between a spiritual manifestation of God and one of the devil? Spiritual manifestations from God "inviteth and enticeth to do good continually; wherefore, every thing which inviteth and enticeth to do good, and to love God, and to serve him, is inspired of God." (Moroni 7:15)

> But whatsoever thing persuadeth men to do evil, and believe not in Christ, and deny him, and serve not God, then ye may know with a perfect knowledge it is of the devil... (Moroni 7:17)

All men have been blessed with the spirit of God to discern good and evil, but that discernment must be developed. You must learn to evaluate truth not with your bodily senses, but by the power of the Holy Ghost. "And by the power of the Holy Ghost ye may know the truth of all things." (Moroni 10:5) When an experience comes from God, it is always accompanied by the Holy Ghost, which will create a sensation in your spirit that is completely distinct to anything this world has to offer, but is closest to what we call love.

Because this sensation is practically impossible to describe, the best way to learn to recognize it is by experience. Over time, you train yourself to recognize the Holy Ghost by taking note of the sensations you experience in the spirit in moments where you lived God's word as found in the scriptures and as given to you in spiritual manifestations.

Do not understand this to mean that the Holy Ghost manifests as a feeling in the body. The Holy Ghost can have a sanctifying effect on your body when your soul heeds it, but it operates directly on your spirit, not your body. It is common for the body to react to the Holy Ghost with sorrow, fear, or even anger, because the natural man is an enemy to God, and because what God teaches us usually causes pain in the natural world.

Always be incredibly wary of feelings and emotions in your body. For example, the subtle distinction between compassion in your spirit and passion in your body can mean the difference between working a mighty miracle of intercession and being tempted to use the Lord's name in vain by seeking or proclaiming a blessing that is not his will to give. The lust of many men and women who pray for God to justify the desires of their flesh has been mistakenly called inspiration from God. Though God was telling them "no," they could not hear because the volume of their bodies was so much louder than the volume of their spirits.

One way to recognize counterfeit spiritual experiences is that they support staying as you currently are. Satan lifts you by telling you how great you are. God lifts you by showing you how great he is. Satan's interactions with you will gratify your pride and make you feel like you do not need to change. Experiences from God are uplifting, but also paradoxically harrowing. When God reaches out to you, he rarely does so only to encourage you. He will frequently also chasten you in love and invite you to progress further through repenting, abandoning sacred cows, accepting deeper doctrine, and taking on previously insurmountable challenges. God's interactions with you will lead you to greater experiences with him and will change you for the better. They will subdue your natural man and lift you up by humbling you.

Counterfeit spiritual experiences are common. You should be very careful to watch for them, but you should not fear them. Instead, you should rejoice when God helps you identify them and regard their presence as a sign that you are on the right path. Satan does not send counterfeit experiences to those who are not a threat to him. It is better to let those people continue to believe there is no devil, that anything goes with God, or that there is no God. It is only when people repent and attempt to come to the Lord Jesus that Satan needs to send them spiritual experiences. This is reminiscent of how a military plane will deploy chaff—a confetti of metal pieces—to distract an incoming missile from its original target. The plane will not just randomly deploy the chaff. It waits until it is in imminent danger.

Satan tends to employ other people to attack you when you decide to follow God. Satan has an incredibly large network of people on this earth who are within his power. When we think of the demon possessed, we think of very extreme cases. The vast majority of people who are influenced by demons are not even aware of it, because it is something that happens by degrees.

In everything we do, we are enticed by God on the one hand, and the devil on the other. What this means is that practically every moment of every day provides us the opportunity to be an agent of the devil, even temporarily. This can come in ways we do not even perceive. I might say something that is totally innocuous to me, but triggers some unknown temptation in another. Of course, this can happen on a much larger scale and in less innocuous ways. The moment we turn away from

God in the slightest, we open the door to demons, and they will get progressively worse if we don't repent.

> 21 Because that, when they knew God, they glorified him not as God, neither were thankful; but became vain in their imaginations, and their foolish heart was darkened.
> 22 Professing themselves to be wise, they became fools,
> 23 And changed the glory of the uncorruptible God into an image made like to corruptible man, and to birds, and fourfooted beasts, and creeping things.
> 24 Wherefore God also gave them up to uncleanness through the lusts of their own hearts, to dishonour their own bodies between themselves:
> 25 Who changed the truth of God into a lie, and worshipped and served the creature more than the Creator, who is blessed for ever. Amen.
> 26 For this cause God gave them up unto vile affections: for even their women did change the natural use into that which is against nature:
> 27 And likewise also the men, leaving the natural use of the woman, burned in their lust one toward another; men with men working that which is unseemly, and receiving in themselves that recompence of their error which was meet.
> 28 And even as they did not like to retain God in their knowledge, God gave them over to a reprobate mind, to do those things which are not convenient;
> 29 Being filled with all unrighteousness, fornication, wickedness, covetousness, maliciousness; full of envy, murder, debate, deceit, malignity; whisperers,
> 30 Backbiters, haters of God, despiteful, proud, boasters, inventors of evil things, disobedient to parents,
> 31 Without understanding, covenantbreakers, without natural affection, implacable, unmerciful:
> 32 Who knowing the judgment of God, that they which commit such things are worthy of death, not only do the same, but have pleasure in them that do them. (Romans 1)

The fact that most people on this earth either deny God or refuse to come to him means that heeding Satan's voice is the default position. Does that seem an extreme statement? Perhaps you think that, were that to be true, we would live in a world where terrible things are done by normal people on a daily basis. It may seem to you that the world is not quite there yet. Christians are largely blissfully ignorant of just how evil "normal" people are.

Satan wisely hides most of the evil from public sight as long as it suits his purposes. Satan is like the ultimate mafia boss. When you attempt to walk with God, Satan starts calling in his favors with those around you. They hardly ever have any idea what is going on. You will not see Satan's power over seemingly normal but ungodly people until it suits his purposes. Consider a prison situation. It is easy to ignore the power wielded by the warden and his associates until an inmate tries to escape. The inmates seem to have a peaceful experience until someone threatens the system. Then all hell breaks loose. The same goes with you when you try to challenge Satan's system, the fallen world.

The moment you set foot on God's path, you will see just how many and to what degree people in your life are influenced by Satan. You will find yourself without any reliable human support. Your church will not support you. There is no place for men and women who love the Lord Jesus and are willing to do what he actually said in any modern Christian sect. It may surprise you to see just how much of a hold Satan has on people who spend so much time and money in what they suppose is the service of God. Your family will not support you.

The Lord Jesus was rejected of his own family, and taught "And a man's foes shall be they of his own household." (Matthew 10:36) Even those who have no idea of your spiritual life will be used by Satan to upbraid you. People at work, school, or other associations will persecute you without knowing why, and make active attempts to trigger sin in you. This may come in the form of unfair treatment at work, severe persecution in spite of doing good things, inappropriate sexual advances, or any number of things that you'd never expect.

This is spiritual warfare, but most of the few Christians who really turn their life over to God do not know what to expect or how to react to the opposition that will come. How long will a soldier last who doesn't understand that the enemy is trying to kill him? Will a soldier who doesn't know how bullets work think to stay behind bulletproof barriers? Use this understanding of what is happening to construct your battle plans. Get on your knees and intercede for these people. Ensure your behavior in the natural world is above reproach. React to persecution with kindness. Avoid even the appearance of evil.

Satan does not work through mortals alone. Satan presides over a host of demonic assistants. Demons will work on you directly (through thought) and indirectly (through proximity). Most people are familiar with how Satan tempts us through thoughts. When you get random, external thoughts of doing evil, this is a demon trying to influence you. When you consider their message, you admit them into your soul. When you follow their inspiration, it affects your spirit. When you die without undoing these effects through repentance, those changes to your spirit remain even when your body is separated from your soul and spirit.

Demons can possess you indirectly as well, through proximity. The Lord's angels can as well. Consider the example of how the spirit of prophecy came upon Saul merely because of his proximity to righteous prophets under the spirit of prophecy:

> 18 So David fled, and escaped, and came to Samuel to Ramah, and told him all that Saul had done to him. And he and Samuel went and dwelt in Naioth.
> 19 And it was told Saul, saying, Behold, David is at Naioth in Ramah.
> 20 And Saul sent messengers to take David: and when they saw the company of the prophets prophesying, and Samuel standing as appointed over them, the Spirit of God was upon the messengers of Saul, and they also prophesied.
> 21 And when it was told Saul, he sent other messengers, and they prophesied likewise. And Saul sent messengers again the third time, and they prophesied also.
> 22 Then went he also to Ramah, and came to a great well that is in Sechu: and he asked and said, Where are Samuel and David? And one said, Behold, they be at Naioth in Ramah.
> 23 And he went thither to Naioth in Ramah: and the Spirit of God was upon him also, and he went on, and prophesied, until he came to Naioth in Ramah.
> 24 And he stripped off his clothes also, and prophesied before Samuel in like manner, and lay down naked all that day and all that night. Wherefore they say, Is Saul also among the prophets? (1 Samuel 19)

If the Spirit of God can cause the spirit of prophecy to fall upon a wicked man through proximity, it is possible for evil spirits to infect righteous men through proximity. When others come around you who are possessed by demons, they are like a parasitic tick-shedding dog. Lying propagates lying, greed propagates greed, adultery propagates adultery, suicide propagates suicide, homosexuality propagates homosexuality, and so on.

There are both physical and ideological strongholds of demons. Demons can also travel through thought. This is why those who watch violent movies tend to be more violent, and why news reports of school shootings or suicides increase the number of both. Thinking about sin invites sin. Being around those who sin invites their sins into you.

How do you avoid infection? You would do well to avoid the places that you shouldn't habit, and treat places you can't avoid (like work or school) as you would a radioactive site. You protect yourself from radiation through protective gear, minimized exposure time, and vigilance. Your protective gear against evil is the time and effort you spend in communion with God.

Your relationship with God is what determines how strong your spirit is. The stronger your spirit, the more you will broadcast light rather than absorb darkness. You must also learn to decontaminate.

Take care that you don't import demons from work or school into your home. As you leave an environment where demons abound, you'll notice the influence of that environment abate. Demons will cling to you when you go into these places, but they will flee from you over time as you resist them, especially when you actively participate in communion with God. Demons are driven by their hunger, and they will flee an unaccommodating host relatively quickly in order to search out a more willing host. "Submit yourselves therefore to God. Resist the devil, and he will flee from you." (James 4:7)

Demons feed on the acquiescence of their human hosts. Prior to the fall of Adam, demons had no need to torment mankind. Satan tempted Adam and Eve out of his own wickedness, not for any need to. As a result, God cursed "the serpent" to eat "dust" (see Genesis 3:14). In literal terms, demons were cursed to have a constant, tormenting hunger that can only be satisfied—and only temporarily—by feeding on the evil acts of men that they inspire. Peter said:

Be sober, be vigilant; because your adversary the devil, as a roaring lion, walketh about, seeking whom he may devour: (1 Peter 5:8)

Demons prowl around opportunistically—seeking to satisfy their tormenting hunger as quickly as possible—and also tactically—seeking to strategically reduce righteousness on earth. Plan accordingly. Opportunistic strikes are something you always have to be ready for. Strategic strikes are something you can sometimes anticipate. If you are on the cusp of a personal achievement or project that will advance the kingdom of God, be extra vigilant against the demons you can count on coming. Sometimes, we pray and pray for a breakthrough with God, and don't realize that many times that will come in the form of an increased demonic temptation. Realize that when you ask for an increase of light, you are also asking for an increase in the darkness Satan is allowed to tempt you with. Be prepared for it.

Do not underestimate the sophistication and power of demons! The strategic sophistication of demons is evident from the account of the Lord exorcising demons from the two men of the Gergesenes:

> 28 And when he was come to the other side into the country of the Gergesenes, there met him two possessed with devils, coming out of the tombs, exceeding fierce, so that no man might pass by that way.
> 29 And, behold, they cried out, saying, What have we to do with thee, Jesus, thou Son of God? art thou come hither to torment us before the time?
> 30 And there was a good way off from them an herd of many swine feeding.
> 31 So the devils besought him, saying, If thou cast us out, suffer us to go away into the herd of swine.
> 32 And he said unto them, Go. And when they were come out, they went into the herd of swine: and, behold, the whole herd of swine ran violently down a steep place into the sea, and perished in the waters.
> 33 And they that kept them fled, and went their ways into the city, and told every thing, and what was befallen to the possessed of the devils.

34 And, behold, the whole city came out to meet Jesus: and when they saw him, they besought him that he would depart out of their coasts. (Matthew 8)

Note how all the demons' behavior was focused on maximizing the damage to the kingdom. They knew they would no longer be able to terrorize a whole city, but they thought by destroying a herd of swine they could cause enough damage to minimize Jesus' ministry in that town. They successfully persuaded the city to ask Jesus to leave. The demons did not directly possess the townspeople. Instead, they worked through third parties (the man and then the pigs) to get them to sin in rejecting the Lord's ministry.

There are multiple ranks of demons. The Lord Jesus is:

21 Far above all principality, and power, and might, and dominion, and every name that is named, not only in this world, but also in that which is to come:
22 And hath put all things under his feet... (Ephesians 1)

All believers in Christ have authority to cast out the lower ranking demons. To cast out the next rank of demons, prayer and fasting are required (see Matthew 17:21). This is not reactionary prayer and fasting, but preventative prayer and fasting. If you are not regularly fasting, you are willingly exposing yourself to demons that are more powerful than you are. Still higher ranks of demons are beyond the authority of most men. It is not our job to rebuke these higher ranking demons, but to call upon the Lord and have him rebuke them.

Understanding the opposition that will come as we turn to God is vitally important to resisting it. Satan is powerful, but the Lord Jesus is more powerful. His tactics are effective, but they are also well documented.

...whoso would hearken unto the word of God, and would hold fast unto it, they would never perish; neither could the temptations and the fiery darts of the adversary overpower them unto blindness, to lead them away to destruction. (1 Nephi 15:24)

As we trust in the Lord, adhere to him, and study his word, we will increase in our ability to withstand all the blows of the devil and his armies in the spiritual and physical worlds.

Seek Ye This Jesus

We know this is true, because it was told by someone who saw it happen. Now you can have faith too. (John 19:35, CEV)

This life is not a passive experience. Our ability to discern the straight and narrow path amidst a chorus of detouring paths is critical. The Lord did not intend for us to have to guess. One tool he provided was the promise that those who are on the right path will experience miracles; both in the lives of those who preach his word and those who accept the preaching:

> 17 And these signs shall follow them that believe; In my name shall they cast out devils; they shall speak with new tongues;
> 18 They shall take up serpents; and if they drink any deadly thing, it shall not hurt them; they shall lay hands on the sick, and they shall recover.
> 19 So then after the Lord had spoken unto them, he was received up into heaven, and sat on the right hand of God.
> 20 And they went forth, and preached every where, the Lord working with them, and confirming the word with signs following. Amen. (Mark 16)

God never revoked this promise. It is still in effect. God still confirms the word with signs following. They include all the gifts enumerated in the scriptures.

If you do not abide in God's presence, it is because one or more conditions are true: either you are not keeping all of God's commandments that he has revealed to you, or you are not yet in possession of the commandments you need to enter into and remain in his presence.

If you are not yet obeying the commandments God has given you, you must repent. The manifestation of God's power in your life can only happen to the degree that you are free from sin. The commonly accepted lie that it is impossible to be free from sin ensures that most will never experience God to any great degree.

If you have not yet obtained sufficient commandments despite keeping everything God has commanded you to do, you have not yet received all the commandments necessary to prepare you to have a habitation with God. If you have not yet received all the commandments necessary, it is because you are not yet capable of obeying them. There is only one way of becoming so: you must become more submissive to God.

To become more submissive to God, ask, "Is there anything God could ask me to do that I would not immediately do?" If so, you must work to overcome it. How? There are two ways God helps you trust him more. The first is by suffering. Moses approached the Israelites to redeem them early in his life. They rejected him, and God allowed them to suffer for 40 more years in order to help them trust in him. Although it may seem brutal, suffering is a very effective teacher, and, like all things God does, is motivated by his overwhelming love for us.

The second way God helps you trust him more is by obtaining miracles in your life and in the lives of others. The Israelites did not trust God when Moses was called to lead them out of Egypt. Moses went to the Israelites before he went to Pharaoh. They rejected him. God provided many rounds of experience between Moses and Pharaoh to give increasingly dramatic examples of his power to the Israelites. At the apex, the children of Israel were asked to demonstrate their newly increased faith in God by sacrificing a lamb and painting their doors. This was a substantial increase in faith from where they were when Moses first approached them.

If you are already at the point of full submission, where there is nothing you would not do if God asked you, then you simply must wait on God. There are many instances in the scriptures where holy men were required to wait before they could enter God's presence. Hezekiah, Moses, Elijah, Elisha, Isaiah, and others all had to endure a waiting period before they could enter his presence. It was not necessarily a period in which they were actively repenting. They were quietly waiting, actively seeking God day by day and moving closer to him in small ways. Every day you should be tangibly closer to God than the day before.

I invite you to lay aside the ignorance and false tradition that keeps the majority of this world—including the Christian world—from sharing in the experiences common to all believers as illustrated in scripture from the beginning of time until today. God lives, and he has not changed. Those who worship him with full intent of heart according to the instructions he has given will find themselves with the same experiences as the ancients—they will experience prophecy, healings, revelation, dreams, visions, tongues, and heavenly visitations.

The words in this book are sufficient to bring a man to know how to be redeemed from the fall and obtain a habitation with God. If, by God's grace, you have found this book, I commend you to seek this Jesus, of whom the prophets and apostles have written. I testify to you that he will literally appear to all those who obey him and seek him. He will come and make his abode with you. There is nothing in this world that is worth more than a habitation with God. Yield your heart to him. Seek him with full intent, holding nothing back. Obey his every word to you, and he will come to you.

Made in the USA
Las Vegas, NV
30 December 2022

64490090R00125